T0198927

MODERN DAY PHARISEE

Addressing Religion and the
Impact of False Doctrine

RANDY RANDLES

WESTBOW
PRESS®
A DIVISION OF THOMAS NELSON
& ZONDERVAN

WestBow Press books may be ordered through booksellers or by contacting:

WestBow Press
A Division of Thomas Nelson & Zondervan
1663 Liberty Drive
Bloomington, IN 47403
www.westbowpress.com
1 (866) 928-1240

ISBN: 978-1-9736-8305-6 (sc)
ISBN: 978-1-9736-8306-3 (hc)
ISBN: 978-1-9736-8307-0 (e)

Library of Congress Control Number: 2020900405

Print information available on the last page.

WestBow Press rev. date: 01/10/2020

DEDICATION

This book is dedicated to the Lord Jesus Christ. The Lord has freely given understanding to share with the people of God. This book is also dedicated to my parents who have been a voice of reason and guidance. I love you and appreciate your continual support.

INTRODUCTION

As a Christian I have endured different trials in life. I have endured both physical and spiritual attack including being held up at gun-point only to have that man flee in seven different ways. I am not exaggerating on that. God has been faithful in small and big ways. He has been faithful in giving understanding. The Lord says in the book of Proverbs that the most important thing to receive is understanding and wisdom. If you can receive wisdom and understanding then you will have the key to unlock yourself from a possible snare or cycle. Remember that when you ask God for deliverance it does not always appear the way you think it will. Some may get miracle divine intervention that completely frees them from bondage. Others get some type of instruction or wisdom that once it is applied the deliverance comes. Sometimes it will come as a course that must be walked out. The deliverance sometimes will come by evading the spot you currently reside. This can mean the church, relations with a pastor, lifestyle, or any other subject that can be aiding the kingdom of darkness. The enemy can use anybody if allowed. Wisdom is nothing if it is not applied. Everything discussed in this book is something I personally learned from a course God brought me through. The glory goes to God because he allowed me to go through it and not remain in suffering. Am I perfect today? I am absolutely not perfect with my behavior. Do I still have to fight my flesh every day? I absolutely do every day. Are their days where I completely fail and rebel against the Lord purposely? Yes there are times that I purposely have sinned while fully knowing it was wrong and chose not to care about the consequences. Sometimes my emotions get the better of me. The Lord knew beforehand what he invested in when He sent his Son Jesus to die for me. However the Lord loves us with an intense love. He decided to pursue that relationship with us. Human patience, love, and mercy are not God's patience, love, and mercy. Many will understand that as they walk with God. Layer upon layer of understanding must be established. We must understand certain things about religion, doctrine, grace, and law so that we may have a foundation built before we understand and address the confusion and error in the church.

PURPOSE

This book has been written from a Christian perspective that Jesus Christ is the Son of God and was crucified for the sins of mankind. He rose from the dead and is seated at the right hand of the Father. This book has been written from a mindset that believes in the word of God as truth. It is written based on personal experiences within the church and continuous study of the word of God. The intention is to free the Christian from the oppression and misunderstanding. The term "they" is written several times. This refers to many in the body of Christ who are operating outside the Spirit of God. Rather they are operating in a Pharisee mentality. A Pharisee mentality is focused on self yet appears as the opposite. It focuses on appearances over true repentance of the heart and mind. This mentality is being addressed because it is a religious non-pleasing behavior to God. The enemy of mankind has harmed many people in their minds with misunderstanding both Christian and heathen. The heathen are harmed and warped from their own decision to reject the Son of God. However the tactics against the pagans are not the same toward the Christians. Many times the pagan is somewhat left alone. He sits in darkness and is usually going to be used as an aide to the kingdom of darkness subconsciously. The Christian who is now in the light and has begun the journey with the Lord is the focal point of the enemy's camp where schemes and strategies are executed accordingly. It does not do the devil's army any good to spend time and effort toward heathen who are already in captivity.

Many Christians are in bondage today and it has come from inside the walls of a church. The devil cleverly knows that if he can corrupt the inside of a church where the Christian is supposed to take in food and water, they can eventually hurt their faith taking in poison. The enemy works in deception. Many are unaware they are being attacked and held captive. This book will edify, encourage, and hopefully free the Christian from some of the effects that come from misunderstandings. One vital misunderstanding is the recipe for salvation. Some have failed to use context concerning scripture and have shipwrecked their faith in Jesus Christ. In the shipwrecking of their faith they cast off their walk with God due to misconceptions they received from the church and from personal confusion concerning scripture. The goal is to show the reader through scripture that the correct doctrine is that the sacrifice of Jesus on the cross was sufficient for eternal salvation outside of your deeds. An important note is that the behaviors mentioned do not apply to everyone. Not every person who is under wrong doctrine will always act in the manners described in this book. These descriptions written come from observation and multiple personal experiences. Not every person who is under right doctrine acts perfect or near perfect either. It is for the reader to discern if these errors are occurring in their lives. If they see this type of behavior or are going through some of the issues discussed, it can help clarify their situation and potentially bring liberty. It is encouraged to review the scriptures, pray, test, and seek the Lord on everything being written. "All Scripture is God-breathed and is useful for teaching, rebuking, correcting and training in righteousness, so that the servant of God may be thoroughly equipped for every good work" (2 Timothy 3:17 NIV). Important points in this book will be repeated throughout. This is purposely done so that the mind can be renewed to truth. The scriptures used and quoted in this book are from the New Living Translation, New International Version, New King James, and King James.

CHAPTER 1

RELIGION

There are many religions in the world today. Many people will think that the religion they are involved in is the only religion that is true. Some have experienced in trying multiple religions. Some believe God is pleased with them based on the works and discipline they display constantly. Some practice religion that does not believe in God. The most important thing in any religion should be the understanding of what you believe. However there are religious people that do not know what they believe in or very briefly can they testify exactly what they believe concerning their religion. They cannot give a full edifying account of what they profess to believe in. This can be embarrassing for them when tested or asked. Satanists and pagans who rely on demonic and worldly wisdom love this as it gives them an opportunity to attack that person from any interest of God. It also gives them an opportunity to exalt themselves for having their own wisdom. Men and women who are not walking with the Lord operate from a spirit of selfishness. God spoke on this in the book of Genesis chapter six. "The Lord saw how great the wickedness of the human race had become on the earth, and that every inclination of the thoughts of the human heart was only evil all the time" (Genesis 6:5 NIV). If you believe the words that the Lord has spoken here, that means every single tendency and thought generated in the mind comes from a foundation of selfishness and evil. This includes motives because the Lord will always weigh and observe the heart of man's actions. God does not look at people the same way we do. According to Proverbs 16:2, God says "All a person's ways seem pure to them, but motives are weighed by the Lord" (Proverbs 16:2 NIV). We have a tendency at times to judge people based on earthly qualities before we can really discern if they are doing a righteous act or if they are even righteous at all. If a person does have an accurate understanding of what real righteousness is, how can they have real discernment? All righteousness comes from God. What does the word of God say? In Romans 3 it talks about all sinning and all being justified freely by the grace of God. If you believe the word of God as truth, this means real righteousness comes from God. It can only be imputed by God. According to Ephesians, grace is the reason for the imputation of righteousness. "For it is by grace you have been saved, through faith and this is not from yourselves, it is the gift of God not by works, so that no one can boast" (Ephesians 2:8 NIV). This is a foundational truth that must be believed. According to the word your righteousness comes from God as a gift. This is not religion. If you have not settled this truth from God's word in your heart, I would encourage the Christian to do that with prayer and an open heart. So what value does religion have in our world? Well we first must define the term value. If you do a search on the definition, you will see that usefulness is a word that surfaces. When we use the word useful, we will use this word pertaining to good behavior that promotes welfare. Is religion useful in the world? Yes religion has been useful in the world. Religion is a reason for much good in the world today. Many religions have done wonderful works in the earth such as freely feeding and supplying the needs of the poor. The Lord says in Proverbs 19:17 that "Whoever is kind to the poor lends to the Lord and he will reward them for what they have done" (Proverbs

19:17 NIV). Many starving children have been saved and parents have been given ample supply of needs in the name of religion. Regardless of the motive the behavior does a lot of good. Religion also does well in its teachings of good behavior. Many live what most would consider much disciplined and usually refrain from doing harm to others. Whether they are believers in the Lord or choose not to believe, the teachings of some religions have been useful in promoting good behavior. The key word is promoting. I think everybody could agree no matter what religion it is that helping the poor and promoting good to your neighbor are good works. That is the good side of religion. Unfortunately it has also has been the cause of many negative things in our world. Many times you will hear a so-called atheist complain that religion is the cause of all the pain and suffering in the world. Although those complaints are usually an exaggeration and their complaint usually stems from the motive of escaping the thought of accountability to an all-powerful righteous judging God, they are also not completely wrong. In fact, most of the Middle East wars that never seem to cease have come from the differences in beliefs. They call them holy wars because the religion teaches them to fight for what they believe. People kill one another for religious reasons. People have done tremendous evil in an effort to promote their religion. We see this in both scripture and the world. If you know Bible prophecy, you know this will be rampant at the end of the age. In John 16:2, God spoke and said "they will put you out of the synagogue; in fact the time is coming when anyone who kills you will think they are offering a service to God" (John 16:2 NIV). This gives a good description of what we see today. Many of those killings and attacks have come from religion. How can the idea of religion which is commonly known as something used to promote good take the complete opposite route? The answer to that question is hypocrisy. You will see that most religious people are hypocritical one way or another. I am even talking about the religious people that take their religion seriously and claim that their religion is a promotion of peace and goodwill. There are many atheists that remain in ridicule because of the hypocrisy of religious people. The entire idea of God gets misrepresented. God is the most misrepresented being to ever exist because of man and Satan. Many remain in unbelief today because of misrepresentation. Have you ever met a religious person who acted rude as soon as you didn't believe or take what he was selling? Somebody who never sought after God or never knew the Lord intimately can quickly chalk up that experience as the character of God. The entire subject of God is now something to stay away from because of the behavior of the representor. Some people tend to think that is how God is and become afraid to enter into a relationship now. This is what religion is in a nutshell. It is a system of misrepresentation of the true character and operation of God. In fact the word religion is the perfect word used for these belief systems. If you look closely at the word religion and dissect it, you get re-lig. What does it mean to re-lig something? It means to tie back. Now say the word again and you get religion. Religion is the system of tying oneself back to God. In whatever religious system there is, they usually believe in a God or what they consider a great person who is God-like and commit themselves to the teachings of that God or God-like figure. The teachings are ways to become enlightened and connect with that God or God-like figure. Whether it is Islam, Buddhism, Jehovah-Witness, Catholicism, they all require works or some type of striving to become something in honor of the God or the God-like figure. It is the nature of religion. Obviously there is some type of fault when a person enters the common religion. If there was no fault, there would be no need to strive or do works to achieve something. What are they doing? The religious system requires the person to do something to redeem themselves or to put it plainly make up for the bad deeds they have committed. Religion says do better or do what the teaching commands in order to achieve reconciliation with God. Now look at the word religion again. Re-lig or religion means to tie oneself back to God. They are doing something in order to be justified in the eyes of God and considered right standing or righteous with the creator. Some religions say to tie yourself back to God you must stop eating certain foods. Some say you must refrain from marriage. Some say you must kill the unbelievers. Some say you must perform rituals. Some say you must shave all your body hair. As weird as some of the requirements get, they all have two things in common. Those two things are works and human effort. The entire focus of religion is human exertion. It is based in selfishness because you are the one that everything depends on. To give further understanding of this I will give some examples. In the Old Testament of the Christian Bible, when the law of Moses arrived there were times when people did not do what the law required. They endured severe consequences. For example a man did not keep the Sabbath. In the book Numbers it is written. "Now while the children of Israel were in the wilderness, they found a man gathering sticks on the Sabbath day" (Numbers 15:32 New King James). To fast forward the man was found committing a sin that was against the Law of Moses. So, as the Lord commanded Moses, all the congregation brought him outside the camp and stoned him with stones, and he died (Numbers 15:36 New King James). This man was picking up sticks. Picking up sticks does not seem like a crime or a reason to be stoned to death. Nevertheless he broke the commandment of God that required the Jews to keep the Sabbath day and refrain from doing any type of work on that day. This man did not honor God's commandment and bared the consequences for it. How much more severe the consequences of a murderer, rapist, adulterer, or a thief? This was the religion for the Jews in the Old Testament. They were to keep the Law of Moses also known as the Ten Commandments. Attached to those Ten Commandments were over six hundred statutes and commands. Does that sound like an easy yoke and a light burden? That sounds like a burden just to remember

CHAPTER 2

DOCTRINE

Doctrine is the single most important element in the Christian walk. Some may say belief or love is the most important thing. I would disagree with that. If they say that God has said it in His word, then they just showed you that doctrine gave them that understanding. Without doctrine how can the Christian believe on God? What is there to believe? Where did the instruction of love come from? What am I supposed to believe in exactly? God surely may speak in audible voice for some people. God can do anything and there are no limits on Him. However the word of God says in Romans that the word is what is required for us to know God. "But what does it say? The word is near you, it is in your mouth and in your heart, that is, the message concerning faith that we proclaim" (Romans 10:8 NIV). Romans also says that faith comes by hearing the word of God. So people increase their faith by hearing the word of God. Faith is made up of belief. In essence all faith and belief comes from the doctrine that somebody is receiving. For example in Islam they instruct that unbelievers should have their heads cut off. They are in full belief that the Jewish people and the American people are evil because of their resistance to Islamic doctrine. I remember one day watching a video of an Islamic Muslim soldier or what was known as an ISIS fighter during that time. He was speaking about the mission of ISIS. During the video he described how his children will grow up to defend Islam and kill the Jews. As he kept speaking he began to cry when describing how the Jewish people stole the land of the Philistines or what they call Palestine. He swore to avenge his people by killing the Jews and taking back the land which was the sole purpose and mission of ISIS. ISIS was also known as ISIL at that time which meant Islamic State of Iraq and Syria or Islamic State of Iraq and the Levant. The Levant was known as a geographical area that belongs to the Muslims. It was known as a Muslim conquest. That geographical area was the area that Israel had occupied. The point being made is the deep indoctrination this man had sat under orchestrated a pattern in his thinking that propelled him to take action. That strong belief he had that ushered him into becoming an emotional wreck shows just how important and strong the effect doctrine can be. How else can one explain the decision to become a suicide bomber? They die for what they believe in because they truly believe what was being taught. Whether you believe he believes lies or he believes truth, he is now going to operate according to that belief. How can somebody train their kids to kill others? The answer is doctrine. Some doctrine can be deadly. It opens up tremendous evil capabilities within an evil man. Another example of this associated with Islam was a testimony I heard of a young Syrian girl in the Middle East who lived with her father. He was a devout Muslim. He allowed fellow Muslim men come into the house and assault his daughter multiple times. When the daughter asked the father why he was allowing this, the father would claim that there was a reward from their god for this act called "Jihad" and that your deeds would increase. The father claimed that this good deed would allow sins to go away and that she would be able to get to Heaven. In his mind he was carrying an imaginary scale that would indicate his destiny of heaven versus hell. I believe there is a video online of this testimony.

This is considered extreme evil in America but in the Middle East where many minds are corrupted by bad doctrine, it is viewed as a good action and is prevalent. When we see high level religious figures caught in scandals and even shocking sins, many look at God and say what is going on? How can a man who is supposed to be the representation of all morality get caught up doing things worse than the pagans? People feel absolutely betrayed, disgusted, and want nothing to do with God. Some will not believe that their pastor or this religious figure has been caught up in a scandal of sin because of their lack of understanding. Instead they defend them because they just cannot handle the fact. Doctrine absolutely plays a significant role in all of this. As it says in the word of God in the book of Timothy chapter four it discusses that there are doctrines of demons that exist. The average Christian might think that it is just the other religions that are considered doctrines of demons. Yes that is true. However it also resides in the Christian church as well. Remember that the devil wants to corrupt the children of God within their own walls. He operates in deception. Doctrine is extremely important for God's church and its operation. Apostle Paul spoke about this when dealing with doctrine accuracy. In Galatians 5:9, God spoke through Apostle Paul saying "A little yeast works through the whole batch of dough" Galatians 5:9 NIV). In context he was referring to doctrine. Paul knows that a little bit of bad teaching can spread throughout the entire church. That means the entire church can be corrupted with one little small error. Throughout Paul's epistles you will see that pretty much every epistle he wrote was addressing an error in doctrine. With the Corinthians it was about addressing inappropriate behavior that stemmed from wrong doctrine. In Galatians he opposed Peter to his face concerning wrong doctrine. Paul took wrong doctrine very seriously and endured many confrontations and attacks because of it. If Paul took it seriously it means the Lord Jesus was serious about it. Everything Paul knew was taught to him when he met the Lord on the governed by what they believe is the appropriate response which is usually what they been taught. Do that same thing to a Christian who has been in the word of God and the response is usually different. That person will stand out differently. Somebody who has meditated and knows that the word says in Proverbs 15 that kinder words will help calm things can react to the situation for good. To diffuse the situation is in most cases better. The Christian knows that escalating the situation is not pleasing to God. They may act on the doctrine they believe is appropriate which is the instruction of the Lord. The doctrine is the most important thing concerning both the Christian, religious person, and unbelieving pagan's destiny because the way a person thinks will dictate outcomes in their lives.

CHAPTER 3

HOW SATAN USES DOCTRINE

Since there is a tremendous amount of importance placed on doctrine and the functioning of God's people, it goes without saying that Satan will attack. Satan is a real being and his influence is tremendously evident in the world. The war is real and easy targets are those who don't believe he exists. It is actually easy for him to mislead and enslave many by doctrine because it is so subtle yet so impactful. In fact it is the beginning of wisdom. In Proverbs chapter 9 verse 10, God says that "the fear of the Lord is the beginning of wisdom, and knowledge of the Holy One is understanding" (Proverbs 9:10 NIV). If you read that carefully it says that the knowledge of God or about God is understanding. The fear of the Lord is a saying of reverence, respect, and marvel toward the Lord. It is considered wisdom to know that God is God and he is greater and worthy of worship like no other. Wisdom comes from right doctrine. Proverbs said that we are to come into understanding of who God is based on his character, his attitude toward us, and how he is operating today concerning us. We are to know his plans, work, and instruction for us today. 1 Timothy 2:4 gives us an idea of what God desires and works toward. "Who wants all people to be saved and to come to a knowledge of the truth" (1 Timothy 2:4 NIV). This is what pleases the Lord. In Jeremiah 9 it says "let the one who boasts boast about this: that they have the understanding to know me, that I am the Lord, who exercises kindness, justice and righteousness on earth, for in these I delight" (Jeremiah 9:24 NIV). In this verse alone we can already obtain knowledge of who God is and what he does. He is kind, just, and righteous. He implements these qualities of who he is into the earth and he delights in them. It also says he delights in us if we know him. This is only one scripture. There are so many other scriptures in the word that give good description of what God delights in and what personality God has. Yes God does have a personality. When you seek him you begin to know him and grow in your walk. Would Satan want you to grow in your walk with God? He absolutely would not want that. That may be an obvious answer for anybody Christian or pagan because it sounds right. However it is important to know exactly why Satan would fight so hard against doctrine. As described in the earlier chapters, religion can prove to be useful and useless relating to humanitarian efforts in the earth. Although there is good done from wrong doctrine, we also seen that much evil came from wrong doctrine. Remember that Satan does not mind if religious people do good because he knows they are not really going to be a huge threat to his kingdom. They may help people here and there but are they ever really going to tap into the power of God? This will not occur unless they get under the right doctrine which means the doctrine that was given directly by God. God never makes mistakes. He knows what doctrine is needed for us to thrive in our walk with him. When we thrive in our walk with him, we begin to see his work in our lives and in the earth. That is exactly what Satan does not want. You must understand the character of Satan. He is smothered and covered from head to toe in his own pride. He is completely obsessed with himself and his own kingdom. Have you ever seen on television or seen in your life a person who was under subjection to a higher authority and chose to rebel against that figure? I remember as a kid watching a cartoon show about schoolyard kids. They were trying to break world records and spent the entire day with friends trying to find ways to break a world record. Well as the day went by one of the kids began to get fed up with the guy who was in charge. He shouted that he was done working with morons and trying to break a world record with people who are pathetic. He blamed everyone else. He then said he was leaving and going to break his own world record and asked everybody who was going to join him in his own conquest. I have also in my working career have seen this play out. It seemed like it happened at every job where some of my coworkers were not happy with the current situation. Basically they did not keep an attitude of gratitude and began to chatter everyday with complaints towards one another. "Avoid godless chatter, because those who indulge in it will become more and more ungodly" (2 Timothy 2:16 NIV). This is exactly what they did not choose to do. The days went on and they grew more frustrated and ungodly until it would get to a point where they would create a plot against the current boss. They gathered people and would basically rebel and look for a way to get the guy fired. It was amazing to see how this attitude would operate in so many different people including Christians. They were not under the right doctrine or any doctrine for that matter outside of their own governing. This is the character of Satan. In the book of Revelation it talks about how Satan will be cast out of heaven that final time. He recruited the angels to join him. His desire is to expand his kingdom above God's and prove he is greater. Sounds like children out in the yard saying I am better at this or that. Well that comes from Satan. In Isaiah it gives a description of Satan's heart. "I will ascend above the tops of the clouds; I will make myself like the Most High" (Isaiah 14:14 NIV). Isaiah speaks about the goals and ambition of Satan. So if Satan wants to expand his kingdom and exalt himself and his ways above the throne of God, he must declare war on anything that opposes the operation of his kingdom. This means attacking God's kingdom and attacking anything that God holds dearly. Have you ever seen somebody who wanted to harm another but could not get to them? So they chose to attack the person that they hold dearly instead. It is a ruthless yet effective tactic that will cause heartache. God absolutely loves his creation of mankind. Psalm 8:4 says "what is mankind that you are mindful of them, human beings that you care for them"? (NIV). In Psalm 17:8 it says that we are the apple of his eye (NIV). In Jeremiah 31:3 it says that he has loved the people of Israel with an everlasting love (NIV). In Jeremiah 1:5 it describes how God knew Jeremiah before he was born (NIV). He tells Jeremiah that he formed him inside of his mother's womb. That means that God intimately and intricately designed Jeremiah. That means he chose Jeremiah's parents, he chose Jeremiah's skin tone, nose shape, mouth, eye color, personality, and tendencies of behavior before Jeremiah could even cry outside the womb. That is the intimate love of God. God does this for all his creation. So when he does this and sees his beloved creation become the focal point of attack from a powerful foe, God is grieved. Think of your child if you have one and all the moments in their life you seen them grow up. All the lessons you taught them. You have seen laughing, crying, and heartaches. Then you look up one day and they are fully grown and being attacked relentlessly. Your desire is to help them whether they are grown up or not. If they grow up to have a deadly addiction to drugs or alcohol and you see them in the midst of their destruction, it can break your heart. It grieves the heart of God in the same way yet with more intensity because God is all knowing and all seeing. He sees way more than we do and that will cause more pain and suffering on the heart. Sometimes the truth is ugly and will only increase existing sorrow. "For with much wisdom comes much sorrow; the more knowledge, the more grief" (Ecclesiastes 1:18 NIV). That is why the devil attacks mankind and has made it his mission to destroy mankind. That is why the strategic plan of doctrine corruption is the mission of Satan's army. So many deaths and destruction has come by it. As Jesus says in John 10:10, "the thief cometh not, but for to steal, and to kill, and to destroy: I am come that they might have life and that they might have it more abundantly" (KJV). This scripture shows you exactly what Satan's mission is and we see it throughout the earth. He has killed many. He has robbed many. Think of the Islamic soldier mentioned before who was in tears when he described the sorrow he had thinking the Jews stole the land and harmed his people. This man by doctrine was robbed of joy and peace. More importantly his will was hijacked by the devil. Instead of using his body, mind, and actions toward something else, he now works for the devil's kingdom without knowing it. Satan's goal for this man is to corrupt his mind with bad doctrine then use him to fight for his purposes and objectives. Then once he is done using him will likely kill him off. Satan is a manipulator. He uses people and he will even use Christians to fight against God's plans and purposes in the earth. He loves doing that because it is all the more of a mockery. Although he seems to be a big roaring lion as the word of God describes him in the book of Peter, he is an inferior being. He is full of fear. He is afraid of God. He is afraid of many things. Often times we tend to think fear is somebody who immediately runs away or avoids interaction with that person. However this is not the case. Usually the most fearful being is the loudest and most active. Pride was Satan's downfall. When somebody is proud they are absolutely insecure. They have a nagging fear that somebody or something will occur that will cause them to lose or take away whatever it is that they have pride for. For example somebody who believes that they are the best at what they do. They receive constant praise but will likely be challenged in fighting their own jealousy and envy once another comes along and does it better. This is how the Lord humbles nations, leaders, says "punish them with the rod and save them from death" (NIV). What death means is spiritual death. Do you see the importance of humility is to God? He actively fights against pride inlcuding the pride in his children. The devil will now work to increase pride in God's people. He wants nobody attached to God or walking with God in humility because that is where God operates. That is the place where Satan's plans can be thwarted by a Christian. This brings us to the place of Satan using doctrine to disrupt that place of humility in a Christian by incorrect teachings. As Paul stated, "a little yeast can work throughout the whole batch (Galatians 5:9 NIV)." As you look upon the different religions on the earth you can see the devil's works operating. Remember that as a Bible believing Christian, we have the truth from God's word. No other religious manuscript can prophesy or to put it plainly tell the future with 100 percent accuracy as God's word does. The man who seeks after the Lord knows these things because he reveals it to them by his Holy Spirit. Jesus many times spoke about having eyes to see and ears to hear. If you follow the Lord, you know that parables were given to make the people think in terms of the Spirit. It is the Lord's desire for us to have the mind of Christ operating in our lives. In Philippians 2:5 it says "in your relationships with one another, have the same mindset as Christ Jesus" (NIV). So with the written word of God and the Holy Spirit revealing truth, we obtain eyes to see and ears to hear. That is why the enemy fights hard to get rid of the Bible. You see many governments attack Christians by destroying Bibles. If you can't see, read, or hear the word, how can one have faith? Those governments know that the opposition of their government is the doctrine that our rights come from God and not the existing government. It opposes the idea of fully submitting to a dictator and his agenda. That doctrine will oppose the workings of a tyrannical government in which Satan is always operating in to enslave mankind. Well fortunately in the United States we are not in subjection to a tyrannical government. We have the right to worship the one true God and the right to freely obtain and carry a Bible. Though you may notice that the government is starting to become more tyrannical by the day in a subtle and deceptive way, we are still free and better off than all other countries. The enemy is trying to overturn this. In the meantime since he cannot totally take away our Bibles, he attempts to work within the walls of the church as stated before. If you look at the different doctrines, all of them seem to be ineffective at stopping men from engaging in wrong behavior. The scandals of the Catholic Church boggle the minds of both Christians and pagans. How can so many priests be engaged in these types of acts? Are they not reading their Bibles? The problem is doctrine. What do the Catholics believe? I won't get completely into the theology, but there is error in their doctrine. They take it upon themselves to change scripture. In 1 Timothy 4:1 it says "the Spirit clearly says that in later times some will abandon the faith and follow deceiving spirits and things taught by demons" (NIV). There are doctrines of demons the Bible states. Wrong thoughts and wrong teachings can lead people into the attacks of demons. In a couple verses later it talks about what types of teachings do those doctrines consist of? "They forbid people to marry and order them to abstain from certain foods, which God created to be received with thanksgiving by those who believe and who know the truth" (1 Timothy 4:3 NIV). When you go outside of God's word, one can open themselves to engage in seriously wrong type behavior. In Romans 1:25 it discusses how the enemies of God took it upon themselves to disregard what God said and believe something else. "They exchanged the truth about God for a lie, and worshiped and served created things rather than the Creator who is forever praised amen" (Romans 1:25 NIV). Unfortunately what happens in many cases with the priests caught in abuse scandals is that they are abstaining from sexual relations without the capability. Now Paul does say in 1 Corinthians 7:1 that it is good for a man not to touch a woman or have sexual relations. However, stating this is one thing and executing it is another. It can be one of the most difficult fights for any man. Paul knows this and makes mention that this is a fight that is extremely difficult. It creates a tremendous amount of pressure and opportunity for temptation. In the next verse in 1 Corinthians Paul says "but since sexual immorality is occurring, each man should have sexual relations with his own wife, and each woman with her own husband" (1 Corinthians 7:2 NIV). This is sound advice and instruction from God's word. God has provided a way of escape. However many of those under the doctrines of demons persist in abstaining from marriage even when they are failing. Perhaps they think that they can carry out the so-called command of God. Many have been victims to it and have committed serious crimes. When a man is not getting his natural release with a woman, something begins to happen. Diverse and extreme lusts can form and now many of them are just looking for some type of way to deal with it. That is why we see so many young children abused in this system because once lust is conceived and there is no natural release with a woman in a marriage; the overpowering feeling can now be a tool of influence from demons. A man must be honest in this situation if he can show long-term temperance or self-control. If he cannot then he should obey the instruction of Paul by finding a wife. It is a way of escape the Lord has provided. Demons love to harm people but they absolutely love to harm children who are the most innocent. Jesus said "it be better for a person to tie a millstone around his neck and be thrown into the sea than to harm a child" (Luke 17:2 NIV). Just as expected Satan attacks what is close to God's heart. Before I left the Catholic Church because of doctrine, I sat under the teachings of that church. A serious scandal broke out at the church. A leader was struggling with a sin behind closed doors. Many felt betrayed, sickened and shocked. This is understandable. However it was just another example of the choice to listen to bad doctrine. Sooner or later the priest should have known that he cannot keep this commandment. However because of pride or because of the pressure of false instruction, many of them keep it a secret and never admit they are struggling. They rely on their own strength to get better and pledge continuously to God that from this point on I will be better. Remember what religion means? They are working to tie themselves back to God. The thought is that they will carry out this teaching so that they may achieve righteousness before God. In their minds they believe that they are sitting under correct doctrine from God. However that is the deception. They think they are right, but they are wrong, but they think they are right. They are right where the enemy wants them. Time after time they try to stop. Yet the problem only gets worse. They begin to operate in lasciviousness where they cannot put the brakes on their wrong behavior. Then that behavior gets more detestable as time goes on and before you know it they are committing serious crimes that land them in prison for life. The devil robs their life, robs the life of the victims, steals the word of God, and destroys the faith of those who observed the crime. Then the devil tries to make it seem like it was just one bad apple and that guy was not dedicated enough to God. Then the rest of the church tries harder and harder to make that effort and they go around in a religious cycle. They are now on the treadmill of religion going nowhere yet exerting so much effort. The main issue was never addressed and that was the doctrine. It is like trying to walk from your house to the store on a treadmill. You are not going anywhere because you are on a treadmill. You will remain on that treadmill until you decide to get off. That is the scheme of the devil. This is just one example involving a worldwide religion and the catastrophic effects of its error in doctrine. Another example is Islam. In this example I am speaking against the unspeakable violence and terrorism carried about by radicals. These radicals claim that the scriptures teach them this in which they are correct. If you look closely at Islam you will see why certain the radicals directly attack Christians physically, emotionally, and attempt to terrorize them as much as possible. The god that the Muslims worship has a name. The name of their god is Allah. If you look at the meaning of that name it means God is greater. Many Muslims chant and scream Allah Akbar after or before carrying out a terrorist attack. What they are saying is that their god is greater. You can see the root cause of their radical attacks. In order to prove their god is greater, they either convert or eliminate those who oppose. Once again I am speaking about the radical terrorists. They have sought out the Jews and Christians. Is it not ironic that this religion claims that the Jews of Satan and have stolen their land? Why is it that they seem to have a sole desire on eliminating the Jewish people? You know that the Jews are God's chosen people according to scripture. Satan always attacks what is close to God's heart. Israel is one of the smallest nations on the map in the Middle East. In fact if you look at a globe or a map, they are surrounded by bigger Arab countries dominated by Muslims. They are surrounded by radical enemies. What is the fascination with this little country of Israel? Why are they the focal point? Surely there are other countries around the globe that many could hate instead right? This is a spiritual component of the war against God's kingdom. In Psalm 83:4, it speaks about this hatred toward God's chosen people. "Come, they say, let us destroy them as a nation, so that Israel's name is remembered no more." (Psalm 83:4 NIV) Many have made it their sole purpose to kill the Jewish people and take the land that is promised by God to his people. The very many wars against Israel are the fulfillment of this scripture. One might say that those people are just radical. However the truth is according to their teaching, they are carrying out the instructions of their teachings. Sure they are radical. The doctrine they believe in is radical. All written scripture both godly and ungodly comes from the spiritual realm. That means it either came from God or it came from demons. If it came from demons, it will be a direct assault on the works of God. If it came from evil, they will always attack Christ. When a slaughtering of Christians was occurring in 2014 -2016 in the Middle East and our own government ignored it, the attack was on the Christians. It was pure brutality carried out in the Middle East in order to promote and establish a stronghold against Christianity or what was known as a caliphate. During that time not only did they kill off people, but they terrorized those people in the process. They claim that it was instructed for them in their doctrine to terrorize the unbelievers. They murdered the men, assaulted the women and children, and made families watch as they terrorized their families. I will never forget an image I seen of what they did to a young woman. After torturing her, they killed her in a horrific fashion as to insult the cross of Christ as to send a message to those who oppose their ideology. Satan is behind that type of behavior. Why is that they always come against the cross of Christ? They are deceived and what happens is the wrong type of doctrine opens up the portals in the mind for demons to enter and carry out the plans of Satan. Always remember that deception says they think they are in the right. In Proverbs 30:20 it speaks about the heart of a wicked woman saying that she has done nothing wrong. Remember that man always has a tendency to justify his wrong actions one way or another. How much more the man who thinks he is carrying out service to God? Remember Jesus said that they will kill you and think they are offering service to God? This is the effect of wrong doctrine and once again it involves tying yourself back to God through some type of work. They actually rationalize their behavior as good. This religion goes all the way back to Jacob and Esau and is described in Genesis 27. Jacob received the blessing that Esau said he deserved. From that point on it was war against Jacob who is a representation of Israel. They are mentally ingrained from birth that the Jews stole from them and they must avenge. If you take a simple and seemingly less harmful religion such as Buddhism, you may not see any error. However you do not see what goes on in secret with some of the Buddhists. Nobody is perfect and all fall short of God's glory. Surely we would not know what the Catholic priests were up to in their scandals if it had not been uncovered. It would have been swept under the rug and kept a secret. Buddhism teaches the full development of mind, body, and actions. Self-discipline is the heart of the religion. They abstain from much and are seen as strong and wise. This is not an attack against anybody who tries to live a more disciplined life. However if the religion is based in pride and the reliance on self, what good is it to God? I am not saying Buddhism is a religion of pride. However if people are approaching with the mindset to become greater than others, then this is not godly. We have seen the Catholics trying to carry out commands that did not come from God and look what happened. Those doctrines and teachings may appear as wise according to the world standards, but offer no real solution to self-restraint. Paul speaks about this in Colossians 2:23. "These things have indeed a show of wisdom in willworship and humility and neglecting of the body, but are not in any honour against the satisfying of the flesh" (KJV). If you read the part about satisfying the flesh, it means against the flesh or against sinful desires. What the passage is saying is that though some of these doctrines may appear as wise, do they have any real value in aiding a man to abstain from his sinful desires? The answer is no. If you ever look at some of the things some religious figures have been caught up in, the things they are doing in secret are shameful. There have been some caught in the typical deeds of the flesh including sexual immorality, homosexuality, orgies, drugs, alcohol and rape. How can somebody from a religion of self-discipline be caught in the very actions their religion is against? Many figure out that they cannot carry out commandment. Some claim that these acts are considered a way of enlightenment. They know they cannot keep whatever doctrinal teaching they are instructed to and now they are lowering the requirements or standards like the Pharisees during Jesus ministry.

Some are now encouraging the wrong behavior as it mentions in Romans 1:32 when it says that "they not only continue to do these very things but also approve of those who practice them" (NIV). Is this something that pleases God? Religion does not please God. Although in this instance Satan is not using these people to slaughter God's people, he is destroying them with that sin and keeping them on a journey that leads nowhere near the throne of the one and true living God. Rather they are caught in their own religious pride and out of the devil's way opposing no threat to his kingdom. They are kept in their place. Any religious instruction in the world that is not directly from God is going to keep people away from experiencing what God has for them. This is why doctrine is essential for God's kingdom and God's people because it plays such a huge role in living out God's plan and purpose for your life. Accuracy is important and we must hear and know exactly what God wants from us. In many cases it can be the difference between life and death. In other cases it can be the difference between a life of fulfillment and an unfulfilling life. In all cases it is the difference between entering heaven by salvation and not.

CHAPTER 4

THE PURPOSE OF THE LAW

If you search the definition of the word law it can be paraphrased as a system of rules which a particular community recognizes as regulating the actions of its members and which it may enforce by the imposition of penalties. Many have said that laws are given to protect us and that in our obedience we protect ourselves. This is true concerning just laws. There are many laws that are not just in the eyes of God. Somewhere down the line they took another thought opposing God's word. Whether a judge or lawmaker decided that God's word was not relevant today for application or they are believers of another religion, they decided to go outside what God considers a righteous law. I think that everybody heathen or Christian can agree that one of the first thoughts that come to mind concerning God is that he holds people accountable and that we have to do good deeds to please him. They think that when they are offered to join any type of organization or religion of God that it is all about laws and they have to stop doing bad. Well they are basically right concerning most man-made religions. We discussed already that the word religion means to tie yourself back to God through some type of work in order to earn a right standing with God. In fact in Romans 4:4 it discusses how works bring a type of wage or earning. "Now to the one who works, wages are not credited as a gift but as an obligation" (NIV). So it is true that if you are talking about religion, they must stop doing what they have considered bad and do good works in replacement. However what many fail to realize is that God does not operate like that today. God does not operate in religion today. The common thought is that God is up there just ready to point the finger at you when you mess up. Or that God is only there to tell you what to do and what to stop doing in order to please him. For those who genuinely believe they are following the one true God through some religion, they really believe this is the character of God. They do not see him as a loving Father. Sure they may say that they do, but they quickly say that in order to keep God as a loving Father or to continue to be accepted by God, they must continue in their deeds. This puts them in a place of fear. Fear is at the heart of religion. As stated earlier, in the Old Testament the Jews under the Law of Moses were a slave to fear. They worried if they were going to sin and be punished from God and the leaders. All worry and anxiety is based in fear. In Romans 8:15 it mentions the spirit of fear that operates those in religion or of those who were under the Law of Moses. This law was known as the Ten Commandments. Why am I calling the Law of Moses a religion? We have to understand more about the law now. The Law of Moses was a law given to the Jews that required them to follow the commandments and statutes written. It put the Jews in a place where they had to carry out the instruction which led to blessing or curses in their failure to execute the commandments. To give further edification on the Law of Moses we must go back to the book of Exodus. When the Jewish people were being led out of slavery in Egypt after God appeared to Moses and worked through Moses to deliver them, the Jews had been so accustomed to slavery it was a difficult transition. Many times they were unbelieving and afraid of the next step. In Exodus 16:3 it speaks of how the Jews were afraid and complained to God. The Israelites said, "If only we had died by the Lord's hand in Egypt. There we sat around pots of meat and ate all the food we wanted, but you have brought us out into this desert to starve this entire assembly to death" (NIV). Their attitude was not an attitude that had faith nor trust in God who had been delivering them. In fact they were so out of faith that they wanted to go back into slavery. They had a scarcity mindset that they must take all they can get at this point. They were actually thinking about eating the food that was there was worth being enslaved. If you were God and you went through the trouble to rescue these people yet all they do is complain, would your reaction be of regret and anger towards them? Well God responded differently. In the next verse the Lord said to Moses, "I will rain down bread from heaven for you" (Exodus 16:4 NIV). It was a response of grace and mercy to a complaining and ungrateful people. The Bible states that God rained down manna for forty years to the people. Forty years worth of complaining and God was absolutely merciful and gracious to them. That is the loving kindness and patience of the Lord. However we are able to see the character of the Jewish people. They are fearful, stubborn, ungrateful, and prideful. They did not trust the Lord. Trust is exactly what God wanted. Trust and faith commands rest. Resting in the steadfast love of God and in the promise that the Lord will provide your needs is trust. These people did not please the Lord because they were not in faith. As scripture states in Hebrews 11:6 "it is impossible to please God without faith" (NIV). So what we see in this story so far is that the way the Lord was operating was through grace, patience, and steadfast mercy toward the people. So when the time had come for God to give the Law of Moses to the people, Moses went to the people and told them what the Lord had commanded. When the law and commandments were given, the people responded in agreement. However their agreement was not from a place of gratitude or respect of God. Exodus 19:8 says the people all responded together, saying "we will do everything the Lord has said" So Moses brought their answer back to the Lord" (NIV). These people were ungrateful, prideful and arrogant toward the Lord. We know that when somebody says something it can have different meaning from the answer they give. For example, when you tell your children or friends to please remember to do something that you need done and they respond with the right words. However the tone indicates that their heart resents doing anything for you at the current moment. This is the response of the Jews toward God. They said they were more than able to carry out these commands. In actuality they were professing a confidence in self and self-reliance. This self-righteous attitude that they were more than able to keep the commandments was what was being communicated. Remember that the Jewish people throughout the Bible are described by God as stiff-necked and stubborn people who resist God and the Holy Spirit. The Lord spoke this in Exodus 32:9 saying "I have seen these people," the Lord said to Moses, "they are a stiff-necked people" (NIV). In the book of Acts, the spirit filled man Stephan who was being stoned by the same people who crucified the Lord Jesus Christ, said "you stiff-necked people, your hearts and ears are still uncircumcised. You are just like your ancestors. You always resist the Holy Spirit" (Acts 7:51 NIV). This type of tendency of personality and spirit has been operating in the Jews since the beginning of creation. It was the same self-righteous spirit that crucified the Lord. So we see it operating all the way back in Exodus with Moses. Things changed when the law was given. When I say things changed, I mean the way God operated and responded was different. The Law of Moses brought something different to what God was now doing in the earth concerning his people. No longer would there be richness in mercy and grace toward a violation of what God considers righteous behavior. This is seen in Numbers 21:5 when the people really escalated their ungrateful behavior towards God. "They spoke against God and against Moses, and said, "Why have you brought us up out of Egypt to die in the wilderness? There is no bread, there is no water, and we detest this miserable food" (Numbers 21:5 NIV). I know that some parents would smack the daylights out of their child on the first occurrence of this behavior. Imagine going through that for forty years. God's mercy and patience is not human. Nevertheless the law brought a change in operation and the Lord would respond differently. "Then the Lord sent venomous snakes among them and they bit the people and many Israelites died" (Numbers 21:6 NIV). What happened? The law brought consequences. Do good get good and do bad get bad. There are now consequences for your actions because of the new law brought by Moses. It is no different than if you were to go out and rob a bank, murder another individual, or speed on the highway. There is a law now and if it is not obeyed, there are consequences. Before the law came there was no imputation for the actions of sin. Apostle Paul talks about this in Romans 5. "Sin was in the world before the law was given, but sin is not charged against anyone's account where there is no law" (NIV). The Jewish people were not aware of their actions being evil. They were so high-minded thinking they never did anything wrong. How can they when there is no law? As it says in Romans 4:15, "where there is no law there is no transgression" (NIV), there must be a law against sin. It is not sin if there is no law saying that it is sin. Nobody would know if they were sinning because there was no written form of communication to explain that this type of behavior is not acceptable. Now that the law triggered a different consequence, the Jewish people would begin to learn and follow the law. God gave them the choice of life or death. In Deuteronomy, which means the second giving of the law, God says to the people "I call heaven and earth to record this day against you, that I have set before you life and death, blessing and cursing: therefore choose life, that both thou and thy seed may live" (Dueteronomy 30:19 KJV). The Jewish people at the choice of following the law given and having things go well with them or disobeying the law and having curses come upon them. In Deuteronomy chapter 28, the scripture discusses the blessing for obedience and curses for disobedience. Blessings such as increase, prosperity, status and material acquisitions, and being in charge of things instead of being a slave would all come by the hand of the Lord because of obedience. In that same chapter it discusses the curses for disobedience. Some of those curses were the exact opposite of what was promised for blessings. Many extra curses were described also such as the desire of your enemy taking what you want, pledging to marry a woman but having another take her, finding a lack of the ability to enjoy anything, and wishing upon death and not having it occur only to remain in suffering. As we can see the law played a crucial part in the lives of Jewish people that fellowshipped with God. Paul in his epistles stated that the people were considered married to the law. It was a life and death and do or die type of situation. The punishment for breaking the laws of God would lead to stoning and beatings; however the attitude was that they were more than able to carry this out. This is often the attitude of today's Christians and the attitude of many baby Christians who have recently come into faith in Jesus. I call them baby Christians because anybody who is new to the faith is still a baby concerning the things of faith and fellowship with the Lord. There is much growth and work that will be done by the Lord in that person's life as long as he yields himself to the Lord. The Jewish people would live married to the law all the way until a short period of time after Jesus Christ was crucified. This was God's plan. When you look at what happened at the cross, we see that the law played a role in God's plan. Have you ever committed a sin or crime and immediately felt this sense of guilt, shame, fear or condemnation? This is what the law produced in mankind. Whenever people sinned under the Law of Moses, it brought guilt and condemnation. If you have ever felt those feelings you know that they are extremely powerful. They can have a huge grip on the mind and emotions. It can only explain how powerful it is when you see Judas immediately go kill himself after betraying the Lord for money. Or another instance is when a criminal turns himself in for a crime that has gone unnoticed. Many would say that is crazy but it happens often. They cannot see the tremendous effect guilt and condemnation has on a person on the inside. It is a spiritual unseen force that can debilitate both Christians and pagans. How much more will it affect those fellowshipping with an all holy and righteous God? How much more the increase of guilt and condemnation when the law points out exactly what you are doing wrong every day and every time? It would not be a problem if people did not sin. However we know that is not the case and therefore it brought destruction and wrath. As Paul says in Romans, the law brings wrath. It brings wrath because when there is a violation of that law, not only is there condemnation and guilt but the ensuing actions could be fatal such as stoning, death, or some type of physical punishment. Many people do not realize this but the Ten Commandments are the same as the Law of Moses. Apostle Paul says in 2 Corinthians 2 3:7-9 that the Ten Commandments are a ministry of death and condemnation. "If the ministry that brought condemnation was glorious, how much more glorious is the ministry that brings righteousness" (NIV). What Paul was describing here was that the Law of Moses produced glory. There was tremendous glory done in the lives of the Jews from following the law. Many blessings and good things came from their obedience. However they could not keep the law perfectly to the point where they escaped curses and many suffered because of that. The Ten Commandments were written on stone. Paul calls them a contributor to spiritual death and condemnation. Are spiritual death and condemnation the will of God? We read throughout the Bible that God is a God of love and desires us to do things to avoid spiritual death. Why is Paul calling it the ministry of death and condemnation? Because that is what it produced in man. Is he saying that God made an error in giving the Jews the law? No absolutely not. In Romans 7:12 Paul discusses the law being good. What he is saying is that the problem is not with the law. The law came from God. God is the author of the law. God is a righteous, holy, and perfect being. In his giving of the law, he illustrates what actions are considered righteous and what behaviors are considered unrighteous. The problem is with man. The commandments were ordained for life. However mankind would find it to be a cause for death meaning spiritual death. In Romans 7, Paul gives a great illustration of his fight and struggle with sin. He discusses that the very commandments that he tries to follow were actually working against him. "Once I was alive apart from the law, but when the commandment came, sin sprang to life and I died" (Romans 7:9 NIV). What Paul is saying is that everything was fine when he was not aware of a law or the breaking of a law. However when the commandment came or he learned that a law was forbidding a certain action that he had a tendency of doing, it caused spiritual death. Paul states that coveting was a sinful issue he dealt with. He first learned that his behavior of coveting was not righteous or pleasing to God from the law. "What shall we say, then? Is the law sinful? Certainly not. Nevertheless, I would not have known what sin was had it not been for the law. For I would not have known what coveting really was if the law had not said, "You shall not covet" (Romans 7:7 NIV). He learned something and grew in wisdom. Did he carry out the commandment? No he did not. As a matter of fact it worked against him. Paul says "but sin, seizing its opportunity through the commandment, produced in me every kind of covetous desire" (Romans 7:8 NIV). What this is saying is that the very thing that the commandment told him not to do made him want to do it more. The law that one might think is supposed to offer some type of motivation or strength that will enable that person to keep it will ultimately fail. These are the words of Paul and of Jesus Christ through Paul. In 1 Corinthians 15:56, it says that "the sting of death is sin, and the power of sin is the law" (NIV). That might be shocking to some people. The power of sin is the law? How can the law or commandments cause sin? Paul says the law produced in him a greater desire to covet when the commandment was given or his awareness of the commandment occurred. Many do not understand why or how this can be possible. You are in good company because not even Paul fully understood. "I do not understand what I do. For what I want to do I do not do, but what I hate I do" (Romans 7:15 NIV). How many people can relate to the struggle Paul endured here? You know there are things you are supposed to do and desire to do. We desire to please God. The Jewish people desired to please God. Sure many of them were focused on themselves. That does not mean they were in total rebellion against God. They wanted to please him and do well. If they carried out the law properly it would be a win-win situation for everybody. God would be pleased and they would receive many blessings. Yet they struggled just as Paul did. They did the very things they did not want to. The law worked against them. It gave sin its power and produced a greater desire to sin. Let's do an exercise. I want you to not think of a pink elephant. Are you ready to play? Okay we haven't started yet and I know you probably already broke that instruction. Now you broke that law but there are not real consequences. Imagine the fear that gripped the Jews under the law when they sinned against the Law of Moses. When fear increases, guilt and condemnation will be amplified once the sin is committed. Imagine how many times they endured this feeling. They must have thought about ending their lives when thinking that they are complete filth that cannot do what God says. They were stuck in a cycle. This is what the law produced. The question may come up now why would God give the law then if it only led to an increase in sin? I think it is universal understanding among pagans that God hates sin and God wants sin to stop or be decreased. Romans 5:20 says the opposite. "The law was brought in so that the trespass might increase" (Romans 5:20 NIV). According to scripture, God wanted to increase sin. This is absolutely unconventional to the common thought of man. Why would God want to increase sin? I thought he was against sin and hated it? Whenever an individual points out these scriptures, many times they are attacked. You can read those scriptures yourself in your own Bible. They are there and they have to be taken seriously just as any other God-breathed word in God's word. It is okay to read these scriptures and scratch your head. A lot of Christians quickly try to create an explanation of these scriptures that will fit what they already know. They try to make sense of it and feel compelled to do this in order to avoid looking ignorant. The fact is ignorance is the open door to the Lord. Stupidity is not ignorance. Stupidity is rejecting to correct ignorance. Wisdom comes from the Lord and we are to constantly seek the Lord for answers. Let us now answer this question. Remember the importance of humility to God? In Micah 6:8, it reads "He has shown you, O mortal, what is good. And what does the Lord require of you? To act justly and to love mercy and to walk humbly with your God" (NIV). This is a verse not mentioned too often but is very straight to the point and offers us an adequate description of what God requires of man. The goal of God anytime people are not humble is to oppose or actively fight against that pride. As the Bible says pride will occur before destruction. If pride can get us killed and destroy our lives, a loving God will actively fight against what is going to destroy us. In 1 John 4:8 it reads "whoever does not love does not know God, because God is love" (1 John 4:8 NIV). This says that God not only does actions of love toward man, but he is love. So how did God love his chosen people who were extremely prideful, arrogant, ungrateful, and stubborn? He gave them the law. The law was designed to humble the people. We tend to think that we can humble ourselves once we are already prideful. We tend to think that just saying I am going to be humble from this point on and change on the inside. It is extremely difficult to accomplish that yourself. Usually it takes negative things to take place in our life that will change our perspective. We have to learn what it feels like to be broke, poor, heartbroken, guilty, condemned, rejected, abandoned, insignificant, and depressed before we can know what humility feels like. I am not saying go out and ruin your life so that you may please God. However there are many times we pray the prayer asking God to take our pride away so that we may serve him better. We ask God to increase our patience and faith. We pray asking the Lord to make us more like His Son. We tend to think that this means God will just do some quick work on the inside. It usually does not work like that. Many times that prayer will manifest as a trial or a circumstance of pain and suffering. If we want ask God to make us more like Jesus, you must know that Jesus was a man that was accustomed to pain and suffering. In Isaiah 53:3, it says that "He was despised and rejected by mankind, a man of suffering, and familiar with pain. Like one from whom people hide their faces he was despised, and we held him in low esteem" (NIV). In all honesty it is not fun to be more like the Lord when the trial arrives. You suffer the emotions of the Lord. Some may now avoid praying that prayer. It makes no difference because the Lord has started a work in you to be conformed to his son Jesus. You will go through testing and endure difficult things in order for humility to be formed. The law was given to bring man to the place where he realizes that he cannot fulfill the entire duty it requires. God demands perfection. He is holy and will not fellowship with evil. Whoever could not keep the law knew in their heart they were not worthy or righteous before God. What that did was made them look for the coming of their Savior Jesus Christ who was prophesied by the prophets. Everybody should have been looking for the coming of the Savior Jesus. However the law also did something else which was also a part of the design and plan of God. Not everybody cooperated. Many instead of humbling themselves and admitting that they could not keep the whole law chose to pretend that they did. These were known as the Pharisees. See the purpose was to humble the Jews, but what happens if they lie and say they are keeping the law? What if in secret they were ignoring certain aspects of the law and watered down the requirements so that they can keep it? Then they would continue to advance in their religion. Then they would continue to hold this position of prestige and status that they felt they were earning. In essence it was lying and cheating. How many modern day men lie and cheat in order to gain or keep wealth? This was no different in Jesus time. At the same time looking down upon those who actually had been humbled by the law and admitted they needed a savior. The Pharisees compared themselves to what they would see as filth. In actuality those people who were getting stoned, beat down, and punished were no different than the Pharisees. The only difference was that the Pharisees chose not to be humbled but rather claim they were different and of a higher class. To put it plainly they thought they were better than others. They began to earn the praises of the people and become increasingly conceited. They were looked upon as strong, wise, and considered holier than others. Imagine how addicting that must have been for the Pharisees. They were extremely prideful having full confidence in their own wisdom and status. So what do you think was going to happen when Jesus showed up? Have you ever been around somebody who has tremendous pride, status, and gets a lot of praise from people? They are fearful people. Remember when we discussed how pride is fear? They are afraid of losing what they have control over. It is the character and snare of Satan. Anytime somebody comes along and steals laughs, attention, or status, the person becomes paranoid and will fight or attack that person. It is an overwhelming feeling they endure and it comes out so evident and obvious that it really displays the ugliness that is inside them. It becomes very awkward when that happens. However they can either choose to accept the new humbling experience or let that spirit of pride continue to operate and escalate.

When they refuse to be humbled, the spirit of murder is now invited and they have a sense that they must eliminate what is hindering the control they once had. This is what happened when Jesus came. Jesus came to become the Messiah that the prophets had longed for. The law had humbled many and they longed for their savior. If you read the four gospels, you see that Jesus was loved and attractive to many. Many followed him and his status increased because of the amazing things that they were hearing and the power of the Holy Spirit operating in Him. Many also left him because of the persecution that was coming against him. The Holy Spirit was producing evident power. The Holy Spirit is the spirit of truth and was speaking of things to come. The Holy Spirit was speaking of things that were hidden or not obviously known. Yet the Pharisees as you can imagine were not thrilled about Jesus. In fact they plotted many different ways to take him out during Jesus ministry. The very people who were considered holier than others were the ones trying to murder him. They tried different ways to conspire against him including accusations of Jesus breaking the law. This was the very thing the Pharisees were guilty of during that time. They are hypocrites. Hypocrite was the very word Jesus used different times in his ministry when dealing with the Pharisees. In Matthew 7:4 Jesus says "how can you say to your brother, let me take the speck out of your eye when all the time there is a plank in your own eye. You hypocrite, first take the plank out of your own eye and then you will see clearly to remove the speck from your brother's eye" (NIV). Many times in the gospels you see Jesus use this type of humbling teaching. Though he was speaking to all, he was really cutting at the heart of the Pharisees. For example, in Matthew 5:21 Jesus says "you have heard that it was said to the people long ago, you shall not murder, and anyone who murders will be subject to judgment. But I tell you that anyone who is angry with a brother or sister will be subject to judgment. Again, anyone who says to a brother or sister, Raca is answerable to the court. And anyone who says, you fool will be in danger of the fire of hell" (NIV). What was Jesus doing here? He was bringing the law to its purest form. He was speaking on the absolute requirement that the law demanded. He was exposing the true heart of the law and the heart of the Pharisees. Another verse demonstrates this as well. In Matthew 5:27 Jesus says "you have heard that it was said, 'You shall not commit adultery, but I tell you that anyone who looks at a woman lustfully has already committed adultery with her in his heart" (NIV). Jesus says here that the act of adultery starts in the heart. He brings the law to its purest form again stating that it is a heart issue and that adultery starts in the heart and the thoughts. What this did was expose how many are now actually guilty of breaking the law. It cut straight to the heart of the Pharisees and every other person who believe they were keeping the whole law. Remember that God demands perfection. In James 2:10 it says "whoever keeps the whole law and yet stumbles at just one point is guilty of breaking all of it" (NIV). In Luke 18:25 Jesus mentions the difficulty of a rich man to be saved when he speaks about the camel fitting through the needle. Which led to the question from the disciples asking how can anybody be saved? I encourage the reader to read through the four gospels carefully and you will see that the purpose of Jesus coming and the purpose of the Law of Moses was to bring people to a place of humility and a need for salvation.

CHAPTER 5

THE PURPOSE
OF GRACE

If you look up the definition of the word grace it describes the word as unmerited favor. The word unmerited meaning not deserving or earned. It is closely connected with the word mercy. Mercy is when a punishment or negative action that is deserved is not carried out when the person has the ability to do so. Without mercy there is no grace from God. Rather mercy is in the recipe of grace and usually comes before God can be gracious. Think in terms of salvation. Christians understand that Jesus died to save us. This is elementary understanding. He gave up his life on the cross to save humanity. God sent his Son as the offering that we can believe in and accept in order that we may be forgiven and saved. Before we are ever told about the gift of Jesus, we are notified that we are indeed sinners and deserve hell. So we can understand quickly that Jesus represents mercy toward the sinner. Not only is Jesus God's mercy toward us but we get to go to heaven by receiving salvation. This is unmerited favor. We escape hell and get heaven. This is grace. Jesus Christ is grace personified. In fact in Ephesians 2:8 it says plainly that we are saved by grace. "For it is by grace you have been saved, through faith and this is not from yourselves, it is the gift of God" (NIV). This scripture indicates that we played no part in salvation other than believing. This means that our salvation came by a decision. This decision by God to choose to be gracious toward us is the reason anybody is saved today. God surely could have chosen a different option such as letting us go to hell. Surely he had the option because if anybody could have gotten fed up with humanity, it was God. God has seen people do tremendous evil with no remorse or desire to repent. Yet we know that God has mercy and grace toward us with the gift of his son Jesus. John 1:17 says "for the law was given through Moses, grace and truth came through Jesus Christ" (NIV). That is one example of what God calls grace. The term grace can also mean a supernatural empowerment. In 2 Corinthians 12:9 it describes a weakness that the Apostle Paul had and his prayer to the Lord for deliverance or to take that away so that he would not have to deal with it. "My grace is sufficient for you, for my power is made perfect in weakness" (2 Corinthians 12:9 NIV). According to the words of Jesus, grace can offer a supernatural divine strength and empowerment to help us in life. In Hebrews 4:16 it says "let us then approach God's throne of grace with confidence so that we may receive mercy and find grace to help us in our time of need" (NIV). Anybody who has been in the Christian walk for some time knows how vital it is for the Lord to help us in our daily walk. Grace helps us with whatever we are lacking. God is our supplier. He designed us to come to him to receive what we need to live fulfilled lives that are pleasing to him. So we have two functions of grace we can understand at this point. One of those functions is for forgiveness, mercy, unmerited favor, and one for empowerment. These are the purposes of grace simplified. Let us look at more scripture for further edification. In 1 Peter 5:10 it says "the God of all grace who called you to his eternal glory in Christ, after you have suffered a little while, will himself restore you and make you strong, firm and steadfast" (NIV). In this verse it starts off saying that

God is the giver of all grace. In fact God is grace personified. Remember when Jesus said in John chapter 14 that if you have seen him you have seen the Father? Jesus and the Father were one. It is in God's character to be gracious. In Acts 20:32 it says "now I commit you to God and to the word of his grace which can build you up and give you an inheritance among all those who are sanctified" (Acts 20:32 NIV). In this scripture it discusses the fact that God's word is the testament of his grace. We know that Jesus Christ, God, and His word are all one. In John 1:1 it says "In the beginning was the Word, and the Word was with God, and the Word was God" (NIV). So we know that the gospel of our salvation which is the word of God written to us is the word of His grace. All salvation has come by grace. Titus 2:11 says "the grace of God has appeared that offers salvation to all people" (NIV). A good question to ask is if God has always been gracious. We know from the previous chapter that God operated differently under the law. However does this mean that God is not always gracious? Many times he displayed grace in the Old Testament. In Genesis 6:8 it says that Noah was able to find grace with God. This was during one of the most evil times on earth where God actually regretted creating man because of the rampant evil occurring. Another example is the grace towards Abraham. Abraham never sought after the Lord before the Lord showed up. It was said that Abraham was an idolater that worshipped the moon. Abraham found grace from the Lord in the fact that the Lord came to him. Not to mention all the promises and blessings he lavished on him for no work or merit. Another example from Abraham is when he lied about his wife being his sister. He also disobeyed God when God told him to leave his house and family. He chose to take Lot with him. Or when his wife Sarah laughed at the thought of God's promise coming to pass. The Lord was gracious, merciful, and even had a sense of humor with the name of the promised son Isaac which means laughter. Also there was grace given to Abraham when he chose to work out the promise of having a child with Hagar. He had moments of weakness, unbelief and a reliance on self. Yet God still kept his promise. We can go down the line throughout the entire Bible where every character had some type of flaw that God graciously put up with. Thomas doubted, Moses was insecure and murdered an Egyptian, Paul was deceived, Peter operated many times in his flesh and publicly turned his back on Jesus, Abraham was an idolater, and David betrayed his soldier by sleeping with his wife then murdering him. Yet God was gracious and merciful. The fact these people were not consumed for any of these actions is grace. As it says in Lamentations 3:22, "because of the Lord's loving devotion we are not consumed, His compassions never fail" (NIV). In fact much of the Bible is written by murderers or about murderers. Moses killed an Egyptian in rage, David had his own soldier killed, and Paul killed Christians. The fact that you are able to read the Bible is evidence that God is gracious. Now that we have an understanding of what grace is from the examples we see in scripture, we can discern God's plan and purpose of today's gospel of the Lord Jesus Christ. Many times during Jesus ministry the Pharisees plotted to arrest and kill him. The jealousy and conviction from Jesus ministry brought on them a spirit of murder. Jesus convicted them of their practices. As stated earlier, the Pharisees were in pride trusting in themselves for the status of righteousness. Some of the most difficult people to deal with are those who are wrong but think and persist in their actions that they are right. Somebody more difficult to deal with is when a person is without a doubt proven wrong and yet they still will not humble themselves. This was the spirit of the Pharisees. They were controlled by demons or what the Bible calls principalities and powers who established this behavior in the land. As stated before God gave the law to increase sin so that man may be humbled and know that he needs a savior. However God knew in advance that some would not. The law gave demonic powers an opportunity to control those who would not humble themselves. This is why you see the spirit of murder, pride and arrogance operating in the Pharisees. You know the story. They operated as their father the devil and accused Jesus of a crime he did not commit as the accuser of the brethren would. Revelation 12:10 says "I heard a loud voice saying in heaven, now is come salvation, strength, and the kingdom of our God, and the power of his Christ: for the accuser of our brethren is cast down, which accused them before our God day and night" (KJV) So with the spirit of the devil operating, they murdered Jesus. We know that he gave up his life to reconcile the entire world to himself as it says in 2 Corinthians 5:19, "For God was in Christ, reconciling the world to himself, no longer counting people's sins against them" (2 Corinthians 5:19 NIV). So we see the plan of God coming together perfectly. The law did its part. God used the law which worked to perfection to accomplish his will. He used the devil and his strategies to murder the Son of God against him. It is through his death and resurrection we are saved according to scripture. This is the gospel of Jesus Christ. He gave up his life in the plan of God to reconcile the whole world to himself. Some are actually foolish enough to say that Jesus Christ was defeated at the cross. Some have said that it was a failure. This is blasphemy from the devil. Of course in man's eyes when they see a man hanging on a cross they think of defeat. The devil likes the pictures of Jesus hanging on the cross because he can speak lies calling it a failure. Satan has an opportunity to lie through man's carnal mind. However he doesn't like the mentioning of the resurrection because it was through the resurrection that we go from death to life in Christ. The cross was the plan of God and is pure grace towards humanity from the Father.

CHAPTER 6

THE FLESH

"For I know that good itself does not dwell in me, that is, in my sinful nature. For I have the desire to do what is good, but I cannot carry it out" (Romans 7:18 NIV). The words sinful and nature are referring to the flesh. Paul in this section of Romans is discussing his desire to carry out the good things that please God. Those things can be known as the deeds of the spirit which is contrary to the deeds of the flesh. In Galatians it describes the deeds of the flesh and the fruit of the spirit. "The acts of the flesh are obvious: sexual immorality, impurity, debauchery, idolatry and witchcraft; hatred, discord, jealousy, fits of rage, selfish ambition, dissensions, factions, envy, drunkenness, orgies, and the like" (Galatians 5:19 NIV). Pagans live like this with no sense or desire of repentance. It comes natural to them and they rather enjoy it. However a Christian not only knows these deeds are evil but hate when they do these things. A sense of shame and guilt come over them. The deeds of the spirit are contrary. "But the fruit of the Spirit is love, joy, peace, forbearance, kindness, goodness, faithfulness, gentleness and self-control" (Galatians 5:22-23 NIV). One of the most important scriptures in the Bible is written here in Romans 7:17 by Paul. I recommend reading Romans 7 in its entirety to see Paul's struggle with sin. Romans 7:17 says "as it is, it is no longer I myself who do it, but it is sin living in me" (Romans 7:17 NIV). Paul is saying here that the sin or sins that he keeps committing is not actually him doing it. It is the sin or sinful nature working in his flesh. When he says flesh he is referring to his body, brain, and the habits formed throughout his life. This means that there is a thing such as the flesh and according to Paul it is wreaking havoc on his spiritual life. Later in that passage he calls himself wretched. Paul saying that it is not him but rather his flesh is not a cop out. This is a spiritual truth that must be learned. When a man accepts and believes on the Lord for the salvation of his sins, we know that that man is saved. How do we know? We know from scripture telling us. Romans 10:13 says "everyone who calls on the name of the Lord will be saved" (NIV). In Romans 10:9 it says "that if you confess with your mouth the Lord Jesus and believe in your heart that God has raised Him from the dead, you will be saved" (NIV). Scripture guarantees that this is the recipe for salvation. What goes on in the spirit realm however is not seen. By Paul's writings in Romans 7 we know that God has made that person righteous. This is called baptism of the spirit. It is also known as a circumcision of the heart. In Colossians 2:11 it says "in him you were also circumcised with a circumcision not performed by human hands" (NIV). In the very next verse it talks about the baptism of the spirit. It is where God takes that believing person and justifies their spirit as righteous. This is the working of God for your salvation. So if Paul had this done to him and is still struggling with sin, is he not justified before God? Yes he is justified because God has performed the baptism of the Holy Spirit in the spirit. God has called him righteous. Paul says his flesh is contrary to him. The flesh is something that goes against the spirit of God. In Galatians 5:17 it says "for the flesh desires what is contrary to the Spirit and the Spirit what is contrary to the flesh, they are in conflict with each other so that you are not to do whatever you want" (NIV). This is the war between the flesh and the spirit that every child of God will endure. See how it says in that scripture that you do not do whatever you want? Sounds like the same thing Paul was going through when he said he does things he hates. He cannot always carry out the things he actually wants to do. Let us realize that if we are Christians that have believed on the Lord and have been made righteous by the blood of Jesus, then that is exactly who we are no matter what occurs after. You have a flesh that will fight you tooth and nail in your walk with God. God knows this and decided you were worth the investment. God is all knowing. He knew the struggle you would have with your flesh before he made the decision to send Jesus. This calls for patience from God. God is the most patient being ever. We ought to be imitators of God. It is good to remember this when dealing with others. It is important to remember that for some people they have spent most of their lives living in sin. They have bad habits that have been formed in their lives. I did not come into a real relationship with Jesus Christ until I was 21 years old. Some may say that is young. Think about that for a minute. That is 21 years of training my body and mind to sin. I was a professional sinner with years of experience. I became experienced in lying, cheating, hurting others and other evil attributes. Then when the Lord put me in a position to call on his name and seek him, I became a righteous new creation as it says in 2 Corinthians 5:17. However what was new? It was my spirit, not my mind, body, or thoughts. Not all my evil habits and tendencies vanished. Some behaviors I found easy to lay aside, others not so much. The point being that the mind, habits, and your body that has been trained in sin is not what changes into a new creation at the moment of salvation. So how is the flesh dealt with? Romans 12:2 says "do not conform to the pattern of this world, but be transformed by the renewing of your mind, then you will be able to test and approve what God's will is his good, pleasing and perfect will" (NIV). Renewing your mind is what is called the sanctification process. We have already been justified by his grace and mercy through his son Jesus Christ. The sanctification process is about our walk. In Colossians 1:10 it says "so as to walk in a manner worthy of the Lord, fully pleasing to him, bearing fruit in every good work and increasing in the knowledge of God" (NIV). We see that our walk is important to pleasing the Lord. It is God's will for us to walk pleasing to him. Another connection to make in that scripture is the increasing of knowledge of God. Increasing in the knowledge of God means to increase in understanding. This is another way of describing the renewing of the mind process. It is important to understand that this is the most important aspect of sanctification. If one wants to excel in their walk with God, renewing your mind is your duty. You cannot do this without renewing your mind. It is good to understand that this is a lifelong process. In fact in Philippians 1:6 it says "being confident of this, that he who began a good work in you will carry it on to completion until the day of Christ Jesus" (NIV). That scripture indicates that God will be working on you and perfecting your character until the day Jesus returns or the day you die. This needs to be understood. So we see how important renewing your mind is in your daily walk. You need to make it a duty to renew your mind everyday if you consider this important. What do we renew our mind to though? We renew our mind to the doctrine that God has given us which is the gospel of Christ. What happens if we do not renew our mind? We are going to stay in a place of suffering and stagnation. You will become a punching bag to the enemy. The enemy has tricks, schemes, and traps for you to fall into. He has cages of captivity for you where you cannot do a thing. They are all attacks on the mind. It is in your thinking. Are you struggling with sin? There is something in your mind that is lying to you. I want you to understand that people who walk pleasingly to the Lord and understand accurate doctrine are struggling against sin. How much more the baby Christian or those who are being misled in their minds? Another thing to be mindful of is that struggling with sin is not necessarily a bad thing.

If you look up the word struggle, it means to make forceful or violent efforts to get free of restrain or constriction. It means to fight against or wrestle. Somebody who lives freely in sin and embraces it is not somebody who is struggling with sin. Somebody who falls and gets back up time and time again is somebody that is struggling with sin. We tend to hide the fact that we are struggling with sin because it sounds bad or God and people might think less of us. The phrase struggling with sin makes us feel less of ourselves. Nobody likes to be seen or heard about struggling with anything. It has a negative connotation to it. This is not how God thinks about it. Remember that God sees you in Christ meaning you are already pleasing to Him. Yet we tend to think less of ourselves. Well that is actually a good thing in some cases. Why do we think anything of ourselves in the first place? I am talking about who we are in the flesh. We are not our flesh thank God, but before we were saved this is exactly who we were. It was not until God came and gave us righteousness and changed our spirit with the baptism of the spirit. Remember that the only reason you hate your own sin is because your nature changed which was done by the hands of God. If it were not for God you would be embracing your own sin or it would not even bother you. You should know that the only good in you is what God put in you. So think of yourselves with sober judgement. Think of the flesh as a reminder of this. It is actually something that humbles us. Remember the most important thing is our humility before God. I am not saying go sin to stay humble. I am saying this can be a reminder when you fall how gracious God is because where sin abounds grace does more. In 2 Corinthians 12:7 it says that Paul was actually given a thorn in the flesh to keep him humble. "Because of these surpassingly great revelations, in order to keep me from becoming conceited, I was given a thorn in my flesh, a messenger of Satan, to torment me" (2 Corinthians 12:7 NIV). That passage says that because of the great understanding and knowledge that Paul had increased in from knowing the Lord, he was attacking your flesh. It is to wreak havoc on yourself and to use your lack of control and fleshly influence to cause havoc in other lives. Another example is somebody who is engaged in sexual immorality. For example pornography is something that many struggle with today. Some do not even struggle with it and actually hold the thought that it hurts nobody. This is a major and subtle lie. It may on the surface look like nothing and that nobody is being harmed. This is a popular thought especially because it is done in secret. Yet is a destructive force that works against you. When you engage in this behavior you are sowing a seed of lust. This is a seed that will grow and if done often enough becomes an addiction. Anytime that an addiction is occurring demons have a way to control us and our battles become more intense. All addiction is idolatry. Your engaging in something more than you ought and putting it in a place over God. You may think that it is not harming you but the more you engage in that act the more you will reap the emotions of the flesh. You begin to have less control over your emotions and your behavior. There is a science behind this. If you look at the brains of drug users, they have major dopamine and serotonin issues in the brain. The dopamine chemical is the chemical of pleasure. It is a drug that produces the same effects as hardcore drugs. Drug users have released so much of this chemical in their brains that they are now in the deficit. Anytime somebody releases dopamine in high amounts or what is known as getting high, they respond later in coming down from that high which produces the exact opposite of the high feeling which causes them to feel very poorly. So as good as they felt, now they feel terrible. This opens the door for the devil to cause you to feel absolutely horrible. Feelings of depression, anxiety, suicide, anger, condemnation, guilt, fear, paranoia, and many other types of emotions come over that person. Have you ever asked yourself why drug addicts are always paranoid or go through tremendous mood swings? This is the wages of sin. As scripture says in Romans 6:23, "for the wages of sin is death, but the gift of God is eternal life in Christ Jesus our Lord" (NIV). If we focus on the part of sin, it says the wages of sin is death. This means that the compensation or harvest of sin is death. The word death means spiritual death here not actually dying. Spiritual death can come in different forms such as anxiety, depression, paranoia, suicidal thoughts, rage, feelings of guilt, and feelings of sorrow. We know that these emotions are extremely powerful and wreak tremendous havoc on that person. This is the devil working against that person now. Obviously the drug addict is in more of the control of the enemy now because these emotions can change behavior. When that person is caught in that web the devil now uses them to attack others. If you have ever seen a loved one controlled by drugs, you know that the person being controlled sometimes will attack their loved ones. It is already heart-wrenching enough to see them be stuck in the drug cycle but it is more heart-wrenching when they consider you their enemy. The person who engages in sin will now more clearly hear the voices of the devil which is the thought patterns that are dominant in the mind. Have you ever heard stories about those in Hollywood who go through severe depression and anxiety to the point where they hear voices? They say the only way to silence them is drink alcohol. If one engages in sin enough they will go through this where they experience the waves of evil emotions and the thoughts of torment that become dominant. It is not until the person resists that sin for enough time that the portal is shut. Sin has consequences. Some are more severe than others. We saw this working in the Old Testament under the law. The law brought condemnation. If you ever seen a diagram of the cycle of sin, you saw that condemnation was the driving force of habitual sin. A person that knows the law and tries to carry out the law will fail and then feel horrible because of the guilt and condemnation. They vow to try harder only to fail again. Then they go through that process all over again. The scripture testifies as stated before that the power of the law was sin. The law gave sin its power remember? The law was called the ministry of death and condemnation. It produces spiritual death. It produces condemnation which is an emotion of the devil. This is why the devil attacks our flesh. The devil used the law against the people. In Colossians 2:14 and 2:15 it says that God took away the law and disarmed the powers and authorities. The powers and authorities were demons. It gave the demons an opportunity through the flesh to operate. The flesh was nothing more than human exertion and will power. It failed every time which produced the works of the devil. The flesh produces corruption. Galatians 6:8 says "whoever sows to please their flesh from the flesh will reap destruction" (NIV). Destruction meaning to destroy one's self. Another word used in the place of destruction is corruption. Corruption meaning to corrupt self as in doing something that will cause the effects of the opposite of what is intended. God did not make us for sin. He did not make us to have depression, sickness, anxiety, and all those qualities of spiritual death. Those qualities corrupt God's original design. Just look at obesity for example. God did not design us fat. However an eating disorder which produces obesity is some type of sin occurring in the brain causing the effects of obesity. That person looks amazingly different once they desert that sin or if they had never gone through it. What happened? Their body reaped corruption. The drug addict looks amazingly different when on and off drugs. Why is this? The body reaped corruption. The sexually immoral addict looks different than somebody who is not continuously engaging in this sinful behavior. Remember that behavior releases chemicals in the body and brain. This means that sinful behavior releases certain chemicals in the body that are powerful enough to change the way we look and feel. Too much sexual release can alter hormones and chemicals producing perhaps a look you would not desire. Too much exercise can produce too much stress hormones that can destroy your body. There is a wage for everything. I suggest you do some research on that if that

CHAPTER 7

RIGHTLY DIVIDING GOD'S WORD

This entire book so far has been a foundation to what is about to be revealed to you. It was vital that the reader obtain an accurate understanding of religion, the importance of doctrine, the enemy's strategies, purpose of the law, the grace of God, and who you are in Christ so that you may be able to digest what is now going to be revealed. I believe that one must renew their mind to the chapters written before by testing it by the scriptures. There is confusion in the body of Christ today. Doctrine is not accurate in many churches. The devil has been successful in his attacks against doctrine which has caused havoc in Christian lives. Many Christians are in the cycles described earlier that the devil works in. What is more alarming is that many Christians walk as they are not in error. This can indicate they are not being truthful but rather attempting to uphold or develop a reputation of wisdom. When confronted many have shown that their default mode is to be defensive. Instead the Christian should be ready and willing to engage in something that could be for learning as long as they test it by God's word. Dialogue is a good thing. Conversation is a precursor for many breakthroughs. Not everybody knows everything. This should be our default mode. God is the author of manifold wisdom as it says in Ephesians 3:10 and 3:11, "His intent was that now, through the church, the manifold wisdom of God should be made known to the rulers and authorities in the heavenly realms, according to his eternal purpose that he accomplished in Christ Jesus our Lord" (NIV). Manifold means many different and various facets of wisdom. A Christian should never carry the demeanor of knowing enough to the point where instead of being eager to learn, they are eager to reject or correct somebody else. I try to always be respectful and gentle when discussing doctrine or faith matters because I know that I can always learn something. I am also passionately interested in the word of God. When somebody wants to talk doctrine, it is for me not an idea of confrontation but rather an excitement to possibly learn more. I have found out many times that a brother that has disagreements about something biblical; we learn that we have way more agreements than we thought. At the end of the day we are brothers and in the same family. We are on the same team. So I ask the reader to do the same here as they read the remaining chapters. Have you ever heard people discuss the Bible who have no real knowledge of it? They say the Bible was written by men and has many contradictions. Claiming that they have debunked the so-called contradictions, they go on to say that it is one big fallacy and irrelevant to our society. In fact there are some that love to study the Bible in order that they may be ready for arguments with Christians who are not well rooted in the word of God. Sounds like the devil working through them right? The devil uses these types of people to attack baby Christians in order to attack their faith which is their confidence they have of God. When attacked they are intimidated to the place of where they might leave the faith because they have believed the lies of the devil. They have no answer to the so-called contradiction accusations and therefore shy away from the things of God. If a Christian is honest, some of the things said in the

Bible will seem contradicting. However we are scared to ever say that because we fear the Lord as if he expects us to know everything already. So we come up with the first rationalization that makes sense in order to calm the fear of the word of God being contradictive. The scripture that people stumble over is the scripture of faith and works pertaining to salvation. Paul says salvation is by grace alone. James says that faith without works is dead. So what does this mean? Which one is it? It seems like a contradiction. Well it is a contradiction. Yes I have said that these two statements written in the Bible are contradicting one another. I know that it bothers people to say that and hear that. This is the reason so many Christians quickly say that the scriptures are saying the same thing. They say that Paul is saying to get saved we must receive grace. Then people say that real actual saving grace produces good works. If there are no good works or not enough good deeds, it means that person never really got saved. So in essence they claim it means the same thing. No this is incorrect and it a reason for such dysfunction within the church. In fact it is the reason for such demonic attack on Christians today. This belief is leading Christians to the very same attacks the devil used on those of the law. Some have argued that Paul is a false apostle and an actual enemy of God because they cannot get past these two scriptures between Paul and James. This is blasphemy and dishonors God's chosen instrument. They have actually created an entire doctrine on discrediting Paul. Some say they only follow the teachings of Jesus because he is who they follow since the teachings of Jesus seem different than Paul also. Many of those who say this are in pride and say this because they cannot make sense of the doctrine; therefore it feels safe to say that they only listen to Jesus. Does believing what Paul says discredit Jesus? Did Jesus not send Paul? Did he not choose him as his instrument? So if he sent Paul that means the things Paul says to the church are the teachings of Jesus. They are the commandments of the Lord. Paul was taught everything he knows from the Lord. In Acts 9:15

it says "the Lord said to Ananias, Go, this man is my chosen instrument to proclaim my name to the Gentiles and their kings and to the people of Israel" (NIV). Yet many do not want to address this because of the fear in their hearts due to the misunderstanding. So now the church becomes divided which is a tactic of the devil. Divide and conquer is not just a psychological warfare tactic used by tyrannical governments. It is also used against the church. Divisiveness regarding this situation comes from Satan. It is much easier to conquer an enemy that is divided rather than united. So we must ask who is accurate in this contradiction if it is actually a contradiction? Surely one must be wrong if it is a contradiction. Nobody is wrong. Let's discuss these two scriptures. James is right when he says faith without works is dead. Paul is right when he says you are saved by grace through faith. The law demands works and effort correct? For example the law says do not commit adultery. This means there is some type of effort on your part to refrain from that action. There are also sins of omission which means good deeds that you fail to do. In James 4:17 it says "Therefore, to him who knows to do good and does not do it, to him it is sin" (New King James). This means there are things to remember that one must perform in situations that demand those actions. If not carried out it means it is sin because they were supposed to perform a work. James says faith without works is dead. So according to James, works play a part. Paul says your righteousness and salvation which is your faith comes from believing on the Lord. In Romans 3:21 Paul writes, "but now the righteousness of God has been manifested apart from the law, although the Law and Prophets bear witness to it, the righteousness of God through faith in Jesus Christ for all who believe" (NIV). The scripture says for all who believe. It makes no mention of works or deeds. In fact the only mention of works is when it says the law. We know the law demands the person to play a role with works. This scripture says apart from the law. This scripture also says but now. The first two words of the scripture but now indicate something different is happening now. It is a time scripture saying up until this point. If there is any confusion, Paul lays it to rest later in that passage in verse 28 when he says "for we hold that one is justified by faith apart from works of the law" (NIV). Paul is clear in this passage and many other passages that salvation has come by grace through faith alone. Can you see the difference between the two scriptures? To put it more plainly, Romans 16:25 and 26 speaks on how the things Paul says were not even made known until Paul had arrived. Nobody ever heard the things Paul was saying and this was why he was attacked so much as to saying Paul was promoting sin. "Now to him who is able to establish you in accordance with my gospel, the message I proclaim about Jesus Christ, in keeping with the revelation of the mystery hidden for long ages past but now revealed and made known through the prophetic writings by the command of the eternal God, so that all the Gentiles might come to the obedience that comes from faith" (Romans 15:26-27 NIV). This scripture testifies to the fact that Paul is preaching something new and this is why he frequently says the words but now. The scripture says his teaching was kept secret until now. There are many that have never seen this scripture and it shows because they either carry out their own ministry discrediting Paul or just ignore Paul. They listen to the scriptures in the gospels as doctrine for today instead. In order to unlock understanding in your Bible and make sense of these two scriptures, we must look at context. Have you ever heard a non-believer quote scripture? They almost always take it out of context in order to fit and add power to what they are trying to communicate. Even Christians use scripture out of context. Needless to say it is vital in your understanding of God's word. You must understand that not everything in the Bible is written exactly to us as instruction. I am not saying don't read those portions of the Bible. Rather I encourage you to read throughout your whole Bible in order to make sense of it. Not everything is written to us as doctrine. In order for you to understand this let's use a quick example. In Psalm 52:5 it says "but God will strike you down once and for all. He will pull you from your home and uproot you from the land of the living" (New Living Translation). Now is this scripture talking to you? Is it communicating to you what God is going to do to you? I think most would say no. This scripture in context is discussing the evil man and his behavior that was before David and God in the land. He is discussing the things God will do to that evil man or men that fight against the Lord with their unrepentant wickedness. Unfortunately some actually can open up this scripture after doing something evil and automatically think this scripture is written to them. They now look over their shoulder fearful that something bad is going to happen. This is Satan using scripture to stir up emotions that he can now operate in your life and torment you. One little scripture taken out of context can now wreak havoc. Luckily most would take that scripture in context. Well if it is that important to know context for a simple scripture like that, it is vital to read the Bible in context for all scriptures so that we shut the door on the enemy from assaulting our minds. So in relation to context there are things we need to know. Who was the Bible written to? What audiences are being addressed? What was the setting? What was the current program? How did God operate in that program? If we read throughout the Bible, we will begin to see the Bible address a difference. This gives us wisdom. Wisdom is being able to discern difference. There are Jews and there are what the Bible calls Gentiles. The Gentiles are often called the nations or considered the heathen. Anybody who was not Jewish and operating under the laws of God was a Gentile. That is the entire population. In Ephesians 2, Paul discusses the salvation of the Gentiles. In fact he addresses them by that name. "Therefore remember that formerly you who are Gentiles by birth and called uncircumcised by those who call themselves the circumcision, remember that at that time you were separate from Christ, excluded from citizenship in Israel and foreigners to the covenants of the promise, without hope and without God in the world" (NIV). If you look at the context of that scripture, Paul addresses the truth of the Gentiles being excluded from the things of God. This scripture communicates that the Gentiles were not involved or chosen to be involved in anything that God was doing in the Old Testament. They were far off without hope. All hope comes from God. They were never in a relationship with God when the law was given. Although Abraham was a Gentile from the Ur of the Chaldeans or what is considered modern day Iraq, the law was given after Abraham's encounter with God. Rather the promise that all nations would be blessed by you as it says in Galatians 3:8. The promises, law covenants, the glory of God was for Israel the chosen people. The law was for the Jews. Are you a Jew? Maybe you are Jewish. Maybe you are not Jewish which would mean you are a Gentile. Whether you are or not, the Old Testament was not written to you as instruction for doctrine today. Remember that this was times past under a different setting and under a different program. We know from earlier discussion that God responded differently once the law was given. As Romans 4:15 says, the law brings wrath because people could not keep it. God responded to the sins of Israel differently after the law was given. There was a different setting when the law arrived. Men must keep the law. Sacrifices were made daily because of their inability to keep it. There were different consequences under the law when a person sinned than today. As stated before, this was in the time of the past. When Jesus arrived on the scene, was the law not still in effect? Yes it was in effect. Many see contradictions also in the things Jesus is saying in the four gospels Matthew, Mark, Luke and John. As stated before, they do not know how to handle the contradictions so they just go with what Jesus says because Jesus is the greatest individual. However Jesus was operating under the law correct? Yes he was. Galatians 4:4 and 4:5 says "but when the set time had fully come, God sent his son, born of a woman, born under the law, to redeem those under the law, that we might receive understand context in the four gospels when Jesus is speaking. He is speaking under a different time and setting. It is amazing how there are many Christians who claim that salvation has come by Jesus death on the cross yet say that their doctrine on living comes from the teachings of Jesus located in the four gospels. Jesus did not offer salvation or redemption to the Gentiles at that time. Jesus had not given up his life yet. The plan to give up his life was a secret. Remember at the last supper he barely told them that he was to offer up his life? How did they respond? Well Peter rebuked Jesus. In Matthew 16:22 it says "Peter took him aside and began to rebuke him. Never Lord this shall never happen to you" (NIV). What was Jesus response? He turned around and rebuked Peter by calling him Satan. In the next verse it says "Jesus turned and said to Peter get behind me Satan, you are a stumbling block to me and you do not have in mind the concerns of God, but merely human concerns" (Matthew 16:23 NIV). It was the will of God for Jesus to offer up his life. This was not a human concern but was a mindset fixated on greater things which was the plan of God to reconcile the world back to Him. Know that the Gentiles were not associated with anything of God at the time. Jesus was speaking directly to Jewish people during his ministry. Another scripture that indicates this Matthew 15:24 when Jesus rebuked a Gentile woman who begged for him to cast out a demon that possessed her daughter. She begged Jesus but Jesus refused to answer a word to her. Then Jesus finally answered her saying, "I was sent only to the lost sheep of Israel" (Matthew 15:24 NIV). Why were they called God's lost sheep? They are called this because they were the only people in relationship with God. She kept begging and asked the Lord to help her in the next verse yet Jesus continued to rebuke her. Jesus says in Matthew 15:26, "it is not right to take the children's bread and toss it to the dogs" (NIV). In Jewish culture, it was widely accepted to call the Gentiles dirty unclean dogs. Seems rather harsh right? But the Lord was obedient to God and only appeared to him he chose him as his instrument to bring salvation to the Gentiles. Acts 28:28 says "therefore I want you to know that God's salvation has been sent to the Gentiles and they will listen" (NIV). This was Paul's ministry. God was now doing something completely new and foreign to what the Jews were under during times past under the law. Acts 9:15 says "the Lord said to Ananias go, this man is my chosen instrument to proclaim my name to the Gentiles and their kings and to the people of Israel" (NIV). Notice in this verse it says to the Gentiles but also to the people of Israel. This indicates that God is still including the Jewish people. However it will not be operation of what the past Jews desired which was righteousness by the law. In this new operation both Jew and Gentile must submit to God's way of salvation. In Romans 9 through 11, it gives us an understanding of why God changed the program for salvation. Jesus had already offered up his life for the reconciliation of the entire world. The Jews rejected Christ which worked perfectly for the Gentiles. In Romans 9:30 it says "the Gentiles who did not pursue righteousness have attained it, that is a righteousness by faith, but Israel who pursued a law that would lead to righteousness did not succeed in reaching that law. Why? Because they did not pursue it by faith rather they pursued it if it were based on works" (NIV). Just as we know the Pharisees of Jesus days, we see this operating under that spirit of pride. A good example of this is when there were two men in the temple. It describes the Pharisee as trusting in himself. Luke 18:9 says to some who were confident of their own righteousness, Jesus told this parable. "Two men went up to the temple to pray, one a Pharisee and the other a tax collector. The Pharisee stood by himself and prayed God; I thank you that I am not like other people who are robbers, evildoers, adulterers or even like this tax collector. I fast twice a week and give a tenth of all I get" (Luke 18:9 NIV). In this parable the Pharisee is seen here taking pride in his works. He even lists them and gives them as reasons why he is more righteous and worthy than other.

In the rest of that verse it describes the publican as somebody who barely could look up to heaven. He knew he was a sinner and he knew he was not righteous. However the parable ends with Jesus saying that the publican went home justified before God instead of that Pharisee. Likewise the Jews did not submit unto God's way of righteousness. Romans 10:3 says "for being ignorant of the righteousness of God and seeking to establish their own, they did not submit to God's righteousness" (NIV). So does this mean God rejected his people of Israel? No but he did change the program. This new way of salvation is by grace not works. I repeat, this new way of salvation is by grace and not works. Your works are not necessary for salvation. Your works are not necessary nor do they play a role in the equation of salvation. We are the chosen remnant of grace that has been saved by the blood of Jesus. Romans 11:6 says concerning salvation by grace, "if it is by grace, it is no longer on the basis of works, otherwise grace would no longer be grace" (NIV). Do you see the difference? If God saves on the basis of grace, according to scripture works cannot be involved. In fact under this new program, God has said that those who still try to be saved on the basis of works are alienated from Christ. Galatians 5:4 says "you who are trying to be justified by the law have been alienated from Christ; you have fallen away from grace" (NIV). Think about that. Those who are trying to obtain salvation by works have fallen from grace. Usually people say those who sin too much are falling from grace. This is not Bible doctrine, rather another misconception in the church. This new program exposes that. When I say new program I am not saying some new age discovery that was just revealed not too long ago. This new program has been in effect since the Lord chose Paul to minister to the Gentiles which was long ago. However the scriptures have not been interpreted clearly and now I am saying new program because the entire Bible until midway through the book of Acts is under the old program which was the law. God deals with us today on the basis of grace and faith. So what about

Israel? In their rejection of their Messiah, the Lord gave them over to be hardened. Romans 11:8 says "God gave them a spirit of stupor, eyes that would not see, ears that would not hear, down to this very day." They are experiencing right now a hardening from the Lord. This was the reason the Gentiles obtain salvation. Romans 11:11 says "did they stumble in order that they might fall? Absolutely not. Rather through their trespass salvation has come to the Gentiles to make Israel jealous" (NIV). God is giving salvation to the Gentiles to make Israel jealous. If you think about that for a second, God is going to find a way to make Israel envious. So how would God accomplish this? Let us remember the attitude of the Jews. They were often called throughout the Bible by God stubborn and prideful toward God. They seemed to have this attitude with God and many times rejected their relationship with Him. In God's frustration with the attitude of his chosen people, he says in Isaiah 65:2 "all day long I have held out my hands to an obstinate people, who walk in ways not good, pursuing their own imaginations" (NIV). As scripture stated before Israel will experience a hardening and become jealous because they pursued righteousness from God by their own hands or by works. This was not God's plan. They did not submit. So God is now making Israel jealous by giving everything they worked for in their stubbornness to the Gentiles. Remember that the Gentiles were disdained among the Jews. They were called dogs, unclean, and were treated very poorly. Remember also that they had no relationship with God nor did they often desire one. They did not work for anything and hardly tried to please God. Well God is now going to give the riches of his grace to a people who never even worked for it. Everything that the Jews worked for is now given freely to the Gentiles who simply believe on the Lord. God is giving the riches of his grace to a people now who never sought after God. Isaiah 65:1 says "I revealed myself to those who did not ask for me; I was found by those who did not seek me. To a nation that did not call on my name, I said, 'Here am I, here am I'"

(NIV). Have you ever worked for something and felt deserving of it only to have your desires deferred and given to another who made zero effort in obtaining it? It is a horrible feeling and would make anybody jealous. Not only that but God is doing great miracles among the Gentiles and working in their lives today like never before. To witness that as Jew would make them very envious. In fact it probably would make them sick to see those who are absolutely worthless and unclean to triumph in their lives by God's grace. This is the richness of the salvation and goodness we receive from God by the sacrifice of Jesus. Romans 11:12 says "now if the Gentiles were enriched because the people of Israel turned down God's offer of salvation, think how much greater a blessing the world will share when they finally accept it" (NLV). Their fall means riches for the world. That is why Paul says in Romans that this is a gift. A gift is defined as something given willingly without that person earning or paying for it. This is what is in operation today. That is why we receive salvation by faith and faith alone. It is a free gift. Let us go back to the initial question that was asked in the beginning of the chapter. Who is right between Paul and James when Paul says salvation by grace and not of works, and James says faith without works is dead? We now know that context matters. Paul is speaking to Gentiles and Jews that are in a different program now that has been instituted by God which is salvation by grace through faith not of works. Israel is experiencing a hardening and righteousness has come to the Gentiles. So who is James speaking to? In James 1:1 you have your answer. James 1:1 says "James, a servant of God and of the Lord Jesus Christ, to the twelve tribes scattered among the nations, Greetings" (NIV). James is speaking directly to the Jewish people. There is no mention of Gentiles. So what does this indicate? This indicates a difference in the program again. What does James say about faith and works? He says works are necessary. This is different than Paul. So the program has been changed back to God dealing with the Jews on a basis of works. Why does the program change back? It changes back because Paul's gospel which is the gospel of grace with the inclusion of Gentiles is a time period called the dispensation of grace. It is a change or exemption of the usual program that was occurring. If you doubt that, think about the 13 epistles of Paul. 13 is a known number of rebellion toward God. But it is also a number of prophetic promises concerning Abraham's seed. You can look that up if you are interested. I personally believe that God chose for Paul to write 13 epistles for reason that this was written to the Gentiles who were a people known for rebellion and lawlessness toward God but also a people of promise. What is the first book written after those 13 epistles? It is the book of Hebrews. Why would God call the first book after Paul's epistles the book of Hebrews? God does this because it is written to the Jewish people. What caused God to go back to dealing with his people again? We have to read Romans 11:25 to understand the plan of God. Apostle Paul calls it the mystery of God. Romans 11:25 says "I do not want you to be ignorant of this mystery, brothers and sisters so that you may not be conceited: Israel has experienced a hardening in part until the full number of the Gentiles has come in" (NIV). Israel is experiencing this hardening because God wants to save as many Gentiles as possible. When you read that scripture the word until indicates that a time will come when this will end and God will go back to dealing with Israel. This will not happen however until the full number of Gentiles are saved by the grace of God. You can really understand this when you go through Romans 9 through 11 like stated before. A mystery in connection with this is something called the rapture. The rapture is what is known as being caught up in the air and taken out of the earth. I want you to focus on the two phrases caught up and taken. It will make sense when reading these next scriptures. In 1 Thessalonians Paul discusses this mystery saying "after that we who are still alive and are left will be caught up together with them in the clouds to meet the Lord in the air. And so we will be with be hard to digest for somebody who has never learned this before. That is why reviewing everything that is written with scripture is encouraged so that you may see the verses and make sense of them yourself. Much confusion has been in the church among believers concerning doctrine. These are not things that are preached in many churches. I ask the reader to take everything to God and ask for understanding. The Holy Spirit will help you learn and grow in the grace of God.

CHAPTER 8

SUBTLE
INFILTRATION

It has been said that in war it is essential to know your enemy and know yourself. Knowing your strengths and weaknesses and knowing the weaknesses and strengths of your enemy can help an army or individual achieve victory. It is essential for the Christian to have an understanding of the enemy and how he is working. The inside of the church walls is the place where Christians are attacked. As stated, the devil has used subtle scripture manipulation accompanied by using leaders that are in ignorance and pride to aide in the assault. The devil knows what state of mind we are in since the Garden of Eden when Adam sinned. After falling Adam and Eve were fearful and hid from God. This is a common behavior that accompanies guilt and condemnation. Guilt and condemnation comes from what? It comes from wrong thinking when we sin against God. In our minds we sin and have a natural tendency to fear negative consequences. We have the tendency to think God will correct us with receiving something evil or a negative consequence. I am not saying God will not treat you as sons and discipline you because that will happen. However the tendency to think that God is causing evil in our lives as punishment for sins or to pay for them ourselves is wrong. God has said in Romans 8:15 that we are not receiving a spirit that makes us a slave again to fear which is the fear of God's judgement. This is the effect of the tactic of Satan to get people to sin. Then sin comes and we naturally feel feelings of fear and anxiety. I am speaking to Christian. Most pagans don't care but rather embrace their sin. We know that the law gave power to Satan and sin. We know that the Jews were under the law. So now is their gospel which is performance-based acceptance by keeping the law, is this for us today? We know that it is not. In fact Paul says in Romans 11:28 that they are our enemies concerning doctrine. "As far as the gospel is concerned they are enemies for your sake" (Romans 11:28 NIV). So what does this indicate? Performance-based acceptance which is not the gospel of grace is the enemy to God's people today. If you are a believer on Jesus today and have a relationship with God, the strategy of the enemy is to disrupt that relationship by misrepresenting God. You can't see God and usually cannot hear him with an audible voice. As the Bible says in Romans 1:17, "for in the gospel the righteousness of God is revealed, a righteousness that is by faith from first to last, just as it is written, the righteous will live by faith" (NIV). We are called to live by faith. When it says from faith to faith it means our relationship starts with faith and ends with faith. This is pleasing to the Lord. Saved is a past tense word meaning it is done once the individual has received. Our salvation began with faith and will remain by faith. The enemy operates by deception. So if he can gain many preachers and teachers to preach a works-based or performance-based gospel and attain Christians who believe this type of doctrine, Satan can assault and control them. These types of preachers, leaders, and even Christians tend to behave like the Pharisees of old who crucified Jesus. Why? Because their trust may have started with accepting the Lord, however they have now been trained with a different gospel. Have you ever been to a church these days? Many operate with lots of passion, emotion, and commitment.

This is not inherently evil. Good passion, emotion, and commitment are good qualities. The Bible would call this zeal. Many churches are zealous for the Lord. Zeal without knowledge is deadly. In Proverbs 19:2 it says "zeal without knowledge is not good how much more will hasty feet miss the way" (NIV). Doesn't this describe the Pharisees accurately? They had amazing zeal yet were without knowledge. They crucified the Son of the God they claimed to worship. How many Christians are quick to denounce the teaching or so-called sins of others? I remember one day when I was attending a church with a childhood friend. After attending their church for a few months I began to realize the doctrine was religious although they claimed it was the opposite of religion. It was subtle and deceptive. It was controlling and manipulative. Sure they put on a good show and tugged at your heart and emotions. But was their biblical doctrine? No there was some errors involved. It was a performance-based church. When I showed my friend the scriptures indicating that we are saved by grace and that we cannot lose our salvation when the church says we are sinning too much, he mocked and became angry towards me. At that moment the Lord showed me Galatians 4:29. It says "at that time the son born according to the flesh persecuted the son born by the power of the Spirit. It is the same now" (Galatians 4:29 NIV). The son born according to the flesh means he was born by works. The son born by the Spirit was done by God's hand and by promise. My friend believed at the time that his salvation was of works and that if he did not keep up works or sinned too much, he was in danger of losing his salvation. God gave me the scripture Galatians 2:21 that says "I do not set aside the grace of God, for if righteousness could be gained through the law, Christ died for nothing" (NIV). The next day he apologized as well as I did for the argument. However did he really understand what I was mentioning from scripture? No because he remained in the same doctrine for a while after. We had to agree to disagree because that is just the way it can be sometimes. It is not easy to be involved in deceptive doctrine.

As stated before renewing your mind is a lifelong process. The Pharisees were all over the church. This is what is occurring today. The preachers are preaching a message that is motivational. It is like a coach giving his team a motivational speech before they go out and perform. The sermons are based on guilt, fear, condemnation, and motivation for the Christian to try harder. They pump up the Christians in their flesh to want to do better. They quote scripture during the sermon; however the scriptures they use are out of context. They quote Jesus who was under the law many times. They claim you are going to hell if you sin too much. They claim if you are not doing well enough then you are lukewarm and also in danger of hell. If they don't see enough fruit displayed in the individual they begin to use guilt or fear to squeeze out more fruit. As if anybody in there church is on their timetable. God works on certain individuals in his own timetable. Just because a pastor wants to see a return on investment quickly enough to settle down his own possible insecurities does not mean it works like that. Sometimes the pressure of pastoring a church can cause either a good or bad image depending on how well everything plays out. If the congregation has a lot of sin, it reflects on the pastor as not being able to handle the job. There is a lot of pressure in today's church because unfortunately it is being run as a business. These pressures grow on pastors and they take it out on their flock. Not to mention already being defeated by believing performance-based doctrine. God is longsuffering. It is a fruit of the spirit. Nevertheless some pastors get impatient with the circumstances as to what their mind conceives as the right amount of works and their own timetable. This leads to sermons of motivation and guilt to step up performance. Then many of the Christians in the church back it up with shouts of agreement claiming that the pastor is preaching correctly. They call it hard preaching or hell, fire, and brimstone in your face style of preaching. This is not right doctrine for people who are already saved. What does this do to the believers today? They try harder. They have fear of hell still. Fear is at the heart of religion. Now they worship God from a place of fear. We are to fear and have a reverence for God. I am not talking about that. I am talking about the fear of losing salvation. The loss of salvation now is the focal point of everything they do in life. It controls them and how can anybody have peace in life? Are we not called to peace through the blood of Jesus? Our God is a God of peace. Is he only a God of peace when we do right? No absolutely not. All the while the Christians cannot show panic or vulnerability for fear of being judged by their peers. When a courageous soul comes out and asks for help, what type of help does he get? He gets Pharisee type help from the leaders and members of the church. They offer pathetic unhelpful advice that actually torments the Christian even further. They claim they cannot stop sinning in a certain area and the leader tells them to pray more, attend church more, tithe more, and walk in love more. The advice given says to do more and perform more. Even worse the Pharisee leader and Pharisee members of the church say that the person is perhaps not saved. Not saved? This is one of the more foolish and deadly remarks somebody can say to someone they call a brother. They insinuate there is no help for you from God and you have let him down because it simply should not be happening. It destroys the faith of many. Then they walk away from God thinking they cannot do it. Well they are actually honest and right. They cannot do it. You cannot live right on your own without the Spirit of God operating on your behalf. Words are spirit. Doctrine is spiritual. Any type of contamination of doctrine is a spiritual contamination which contaminates faith. We want the truth of God's word for us today. Paul struggled with sin under the right doctrine, how much more will Christians struggle today with wrong doctrine? At least these Christians or former Christians are honest enough to admit it. However the Pharisee leaders and Pharisee Christians are not being honest. They preach a doctrine of works and motivational speeches that they don't even live by. Everyone in a church that preaches like that and treats Christians like that should be humbled and come together to admit they are blowing it in one area or another. The problem is they are mixing both law and grace. They water down the law enough to where they are thinking that they are keeping it, all the while taking in grace for the daily flaws. This produces a Pharisee attitude and culture in God's church. The true law would completely humble them to the point of desperately desiring grace. They would be more grateful for the grace and mercy of God. Yet because the requirements are lowered, they don't think they have much to correct and almost automatically become arrogant and confident in themselves. They think their way of operation is actually effective because they don't see their own sin as much which is what would move a Christian to depend on God more. If they are not admitting this then they are doing one of two things. They are hiding their sin or they honestly believe they are doing enough to stay saved. They are still operating with the imaginary scale of good and bad deeds. They believe the gospel is a message that says Jesus did his part to save us, now we must do our part. And what happens when they see others not bearing enough fruit? They lay a guilt trip on them saying God died for you and you cannot stop sinning in this area? You cannot give that up for God? Accountability is an acceptable principle. Guilt and condemnation in an attempt to change somebody's behavior is a witchcraft tactic. It is a device used to control people. How many people have you heard claim religion is nothing more than a means of controlling people and making money? They are right in many situations including the way many people of the Christian church have operated. This is not of God. When the Lord showed me this, the book of Galatians was the book of understanding for me. If you read Galatians, it is a book that addresses this issue of performance-based acceptance. The Galatians had been saved by grace. However there were teachers claiming you have to keep the law to stay saved. Is this not something that is occurring today? Keep a good amount of works to stay saved or you may lose your salvation. Galatians 3:2 says

"I would like to learn just one thing from you: Did you receive the Spirit by the works of the law, or by believing what you heard? Did you get saved by doing works or by believing the gospel? Are you so foolish, after beginning by means of the Spirit are you now trying to finish by means of the flesh" (NIV). Are you trying to stay saved by mere effort or your own works? This is performance-based acceptance. Paul continues saying "so again I ask does God give you his Spirit and work miracles among you by the works of the law, or by your believing what you heard" (NIV). Does God have a relationship with you, love you, and do good things to you because you do good works or sustain a certain amount of good works, or because you believe the message of grace which was his decision to provide a way of salvation by believing on his Son Jesus? These scriptures are shields to the enemy's attacks. As the Bible says in Ephesians 6, the word of God is a shield and it quenches the fiery darts of the enemy. Pastors and our fellow Christians have attacked those who believe that we are saved by grace alone and will remain saved by grace alone. They throw the scriptures at them of Jesus who was under the law. Then when confronted, they say they only follow Jesus and you are not following God because you are following what Paul wrote. They fail to rightly divide God's word in context. They come at you with legalism. Remember that the devil is the accuser of the brethren and scripture says he accuses us day and night. So when you tell them scripture, that spirit of self-righteousness that works in them will always look to talk its way out of the situation. This is the behavior of narcissists. They love to win arguments and be able to escape all accountability. They love the fact that through smooth talk they can be wrong yet manipulate their way into seeming right. This is of the devil. I am not saying all Christians who are under the performance-based acceptance doctrine are like this. I am saying if this is what you see happening in the church, it must be addressed. Everyone must examine themselves with honesty. In Revelation 3 it discusses a lukewarm church. "So, because you are lukewarm meaning neither hot nor cold, I am about to spit you out of my mouth" (Revelation 3:16 NIV). Many legalistic Christians use this scripture to exalt themselves and put down others. In fact they use this scripture to claim many have lost their salvation. If you are lukewarm which means not hot enough for God, you are going to be spit out of the mouth of Jesus. What does hot enough look like? How many sins does one commit for them to not be considered hot enough anymore? How many sins before we are not saved? How will I know if I lost my salvation now? They can never answer these questions with assurance. It is funny though how they claim that whatever they are doing is considered hot enough. They rarely go around admitting they are not hot enough and they have lost their salvation. Did not Paul ask in Romans 2:21 those who preach against stealing, do you steal? This is a situation now where Christians go into worship not only in fear but are trying to earn the praise of their peers and pastors to insinuate they are not lukewarm anymore. They are working harder to show themselves approved in ignorance to the fact that Jesus sacrifice at the cross is what saves them and keeps them saved. That scripture of being lukewarm is speaking to the future church to the Jewish flock of the future. It is not speaking to us as doctrine or instruction for today. Many go into prayer and giving much more than they want to because they are under compulsion. God loves a cheerful giver, not one controlled and manipulated by fear. I have seen a preacher use this against their congregation. Many were increasing their offering sizes in giving. You would think this would be worthy of encouragement. Yet the leader went on to say that many are still lukewarm and this is deceptive. He claimed many were lukewarm regardless and that their decision to increase the offering size was proof that they were lukewarm if that makes any sense. It was a cynical and mocking word aimed to discredit their good work and to keep the flock in check. Whether this is willful deception by pastors or just from bad doctrine, it is wrong. Although the people were manipulated by fear to give more, the preacher used the tactic of a lawyer to accuse them of doing something wrong even when they did something right. This is what the law did. It brought condemnation. When the Jews did good and kept the law, the law said nothing. When they messed up it immediately pointed out of their mistakes. Many in the church are operating like this. Those are the worst people to be around. You can do nothing right in their sight. This is of the devil. Those under the works doctrine love to argue because it holds a place for them to appear wise and profess wisdom of the scriptures. Romans 16:18 says "for such people are not serving our Lord Christ, but their own appetites. By smooth talk and flattery they deceive the minds of naive people" (Romans 16:18 NIV). We are instructed not to behave like this. 1 Corinthians 2:1 says "when I came to you, I did not come with eloquence or human wisdom as I proclaimed to you the testimony about God" (NIV). Not even Paul who knew more than anybody at that time acted this way. Many mock those who preach salvation by grace because it is a simple clear message that man plays no part in besides faith or belief. Those who do want status, praise, and a good appearance among others usually attack the message. They consider it foolishness. 1 Corinthians 1:18 says "for the message of the cross is foolishness to those who are perishing but to us who are being saved it is the power of God" (NIV). This was speaking to pagans who reject Christ. However this applies to those who reject the gospel of grace which is also Christ. The flesh is always against Christ. The flesh wants something to do and something to boast about. Many are caught in the cycle of guilt, condemnation and sin that is destroying their faith and life because of this behavior in the church. Once you begin to understand truth and the enemy's tactics, you can defend yourself and fight back. That is why the Bible calls the word the shield of faith. It is by knowledge we fight back. It is without knowledge we are destroyed as Hosea says. You cannot do better until you know better.

CHAPTER 9

SUFFICIENCY

The Pharisees of today are the same Pharisees Jesus and Paul dealt with. Luckily for us Christians who are a target of the devil, we do not have to act like there is some new tactic that the enemy has to use to deceive us. He uses the same tactics because they work. Jesus dealt with the Pharisees and so did Paul. When Paul started his ministry, he fought against the works doctrine. In Acts 15:5 it says "then some of the believers who belonged to the party of the Pharisees stood up and said, the Gentiles must be circumcised and required to keep the Law of Moses" (NIV). As you read this passage which I greatly encourage the reader to read, you will see that it was the Pharisees trying to take the new Christians back to works in order to stay saved. Peter addressed this saying to the Pharisees "now then why do you try to test God by putting on the necks of Gentiles a yoke that neither we nor our ancestors have been able to bear" (Acts 15:10 NIV). What yoke was he talking about? It was the yoke of the law. What is the law today? It is performance-based acceptance. It is the act of keeping salvation. If they could not bear that yoke what makes you think you can? It is of arrogance to think this. He goes on to say "we believe it is through the grace of our Lord Jesus that we are saved just as they are" (Acts 15:11 NIV). If you read that passage in your Bible the word no may have an exclamation point to indicate the vehement disapproval of what the Pharisees were trying to do. Why is this a big deal to God? Well think of it this way. We know that it is an opportunity for the enemy to keep people in bondage through the cycle of sin and condemnation. However another reason God hates this mixture of law and grace is because it is a doctrine of arrogance. Think of the pain and suffering Jesus went through on your behalf? I am not saying to feel guilty about anything you do wrong in your life to make you behave better as the church has done. However I am saying Jesus went through hell to save you. How much of an insult is it to God when men walk around claiming Jesus did not do enough in his sacrifice and they have to take the torch and keep their salvation with good works? It is an insult to the Spirit of grace. More importantly it robs the man of experiencing the effects of grace that Jesus paid on the cross. Have you ever had a person in your life completely fail in whatever task they were trying to accomplish and you come along and help them out? You turn their ashes into beauty and yet they are so prideful to not only deny you credit, but attempt to take credit? It is disgusting. How much more disgusting is it for the people who God saved with the precious blood of Jesus to operate in a doctrine saying works are necessary to add to the cross of Christ. I am saying this from God's viewpoint where people were already prideful and remained prideful after receiving Christ. It is wrong to think that you are helping God or living for God. People did not have a choice or a capability unless they wanted to go to hell. Man cannot do anything on his own. If a man acts as if he is taking the torch, man gets glory. This insinuates that Christ's sacrifice was not sufficient. Nobody suffered and went through more than Christ. He knew you would sin after salvation. In fact nobody got saved until after he was crucified. Your future sins are paid for. But many argue that they lost salvation. Well how do you get it back? Does it take more works or effort? How many sins does it take?

Once again they will fail to provide a precise answer. Their argument is that Christ is not sufficient. This your entire fight of faith. Everything I have stated in this book so far has led up to this truth and next statement. Christ is sufficient. The Pharisee attitude in the church today is an attack on the sufficiency of Christ. This is why the Bible says to stand firm in your faith. 1 Corinthians 16:13 says "be on your guard stand firm in the faith, be courageous and be strong" (NIV). What is your faith being rooted in? It is faith in the sufficiency of Jesus Christ and his sacrifice on the cross to make one righteous in the sight of God. This gives us peace and strength to stand firm. The Christians who do not understand this are the ones tossed back and forth. They are up one day and down the next based how well they perform. If they resist certain sins and carry out good works for a few weeks, they are more confident and happier because they think they are pleasing God more. Once they begin to miss the mark a few times they start to feel down again and ashamed. It is no different than the highs and lows of an addict. They feel happier and more confident when they have the substance. Whenever you see immediate highs and lows back and forth you can be sure the enemy is involved. God wants faith and rest in Jesus. For the Christian the confidence is in their performance and it drops when the performance drops. This is not the life of peace God has called us to. This is why the enemy attacks the message that Christ is sufficient. This is the devil trying to delegitimize the victory of the cross and the big giant loss he took. Have you ever been in a competition that you won, yet even after you won they attempt to make it seem like that it was not all that great including lying about certain details? You see this in the news media and sports media where one team with a bigger market wins and they make a huge deal for weeks. Yet if the smaller market team wins, the media will quickly get over it and stop coverage so they can move on to something else they can profit greater from. This is what the devil is doing today. He is on a disinformation and delegitimizing campaign in an attempt to keep Christians away from the power of God. He wants Christians working in their own power. With the deception that there is gain in doing this by achieving a good stance with God and being highly esteemed among people, they trade in the power of God. In doing this they attack the sufficiency of Christ. Sure their messages may seem full of wisdom and their speech smooth and eloquent, but operating in their so-called wisdom they are attacking Christ. Colossians 2 says "see to it that no one takes you captive through hollow and deceptive philosophy, which depends on human tradition and the basic principles of this world rather than on Christ" (NIV). All the attack is against the sufficiency of Christ. Colossians 2:10 says we are complete in Christ. If you notice a pattern in Paul's epistles, he first addresses doctrine in the early chapters that speak on the sufficiency of Christ. He then encourages walking in that sufficiency knowing that God has made us complete in Him. If we are made complete, we cannot add to what God has done. This is concerning justification or salvation. In sanctification which is our daily walk, we can rely on God to mold our character. We are encouraged to cooperate and avoid sin because it is detrimental to our growth. However the word doesn't tell us that we lose salvation when we sin as many false teachers do. As you see in the book of 1 Corinthians, Paul was addressing sin in the church. There was a man having sex with his father's wife. Whether this was incest or if this was the stepmother is not known to me. Nevertheless this sin is a very detestable act regardless. Paul openly rebukes the sin as something that pagans do not even do. I encourage the reader to read this passage. Yet Paul does not say they are not saved. Instead he rebukes the people of the church that engaged in this act. He also rebukes the members boasting that they could get away with it because of God's grace. He goes further to say to disassociate with these people and expel him. Yet he does not say they are not saved. He even tells them they were washed and sanctified by Christ. Therefore they should refrain from that type of behavior. In the next Corinthians book, Paul talks about their repentance. Did you see what took place? Paul condemned the act as ungodly. However he did not say those people are not saved nor have they lost salvation. How many would right away say this in today's church if it were open in the public. How many would look at these people with disgust and not fellowship with them anymore? When Paul said to expel the people, he was saying that if they refused to repent and accept the fact their behavior was ungodly, they should be expelled. Yet in the next book he says they are made clean and are encouraged to walk in the light of Christ. Paul taught them who their true identity in Christ was and they repented. The sacrifice of the cross was sufficient to keep these folks saved after committing a disgusting act such as this. What if they were to do it again? The cross is still sufficient. Many claim the gospel of grace is a license to sin. The truth is you don't need a license to sin since we all have been sinning without one anyway. In fact many came to Paul with the question claiming Paul was promoting sin. They said shall we continue in sin that grace may abound? If the question or accusation ever comes up that you are promoting sin, you are preaching it correctly. That question should come up. But what does Paul say? Paul says absolutely not. Read Romans 6. Paul then goes on to tell about the fact that the God of grace has placed you in the cage of righteousness now. I use the word cage because the passage talks about slaves. You are now a slave to righteousness now that you have been justified. Why would anybody in their right mind want to go back to sinning? If anybody does think that it would be good now, they obviously do not have an understanding of sin. They must crave sin. Sure we all have to deal with the cravings of our flesh. However for the man who says that you are giving license to sin, why do they hold sin on a pedestal? As if sin is a treasure and committing sin and having grace take care of it would be delight? They obviously do not understand the tremendous havoc sin can cause in your life. In many ways those who argue against through that. I learned many things and now can take what I have learned and pass it on. My advice to the reader is to renew your mind to the scriptures of Paul since they are written to us today. Also get an understanding of the four gospels and the Old Testament. As it says in Romans 15:4, "for whatsoever things were written aforetime were written for our learning that we through patience and comfort of the scriptures might have hope" (NIV). Do not disregard any scripture. We can learn and gain from every word that comes from God. Faith is confidence. Faith is increased by hearing, believing and renewing your mind to the word. If you desire to confront any leader or brother or sister in the body of Christ who is engaged in performance-based acceptance, know that it is not your job to convince them. It is the duty of the Holy Spirit to reveal truth to them. If they reject the gospel of grace, I recommend leaving that church. For many churches are not preaching sound doctrine but rather are putting on a religious entertainment show and operating a business. If your pastor is misled, notify him. If he rejects harshly or gently, that is not your fault. You have to get away though from that doctrine. You have to walk in truth otherwise you will suffer because of the company you keep. Know that their mindset is not your mindset. They are of a different mindset. Their mindset is that they are enduring something difficult to earn salvation. They are similar to those who boast of the hard times they overcame to be where they are today. It is a boasting on self. I am talking about those in pride. Encouragement of overcoming hard times is different. Competing with one another whose life was harder and who is a stronger overcomer is pride. Grace is attacked because of pride. When you present grace in its truth, they claim you are an escape artist and just want an easy life. When you speak on the rapture, they claim you are an escapist and don't want to be a warrior for Christ. It is no different with worldly people who say that those who preach against homosexuality are anti-gay. It is usually some accusation. We should understand that all salvation is prospering now in the stance we are now in? Is not death unto life prosperity? If we went from hell to heaven and zero hope to many great promises, is that not prosperity? Are finances evil? Is it ungodly to be rich? Their judgement or so-called discernment usually comes from whatever position they are currently in. If they have money, they may claim it is okay and God has blessed them. If they don't have money, they may claim they are suffering for God and given it up for the sake of God all while attacking everybody else who is rich. I am not saying this fits the bill for everybody. I am simply calling for discernment in whatever situation. You cannot adjust scripture to fit what your life looks like to claim you are living correctly. We are called to peace and correct sound teaching. Are we not allowed to enjoy life? Can I be happy although I have some sin tendencies that God is still working on in my life? Is that not allowed? God has already dealt with sin on the cross. It was paid for in full. Many come to Christians claiming the gospel is hyper grace. They say if you preach salvation by faith alone with no works required (which is what Paul preached), that is hyper grace or giving license. There is no such thing as God's true grace being false. God's grace is hyper. The huge discrepancy between our sinfulness and God's rich kindness makes it hyper. False grace says go sin against God freely. If they mean that hyper grace teaches us to go sin freely, then I agree that is wrong teaching. True grace says you are empowered to live above sin. Most agree with that but as soon as they see too much sin, they pull out the lost your salvation card or hyper grace term showing that they are not rooted in the true gospel. Their heart is following performance-based Christianity. Anybody who follows this behavior still has too much confidence in their flesh. They haven't come to an understanding of just how bad they were and how good God has been to us. While we were still sinners, Christ died for us as scripture says. Think about that for a minute. The rapist, the murderer, the child-murderer, the pedophile, the man who does all these things with an

FINAL THOUGHTS

God did not give us his word so that we may be confused. Confusion has created division and division has created weakness. Not everything in the Bible is written to us for instruction. Rightly dividing God's word and understanding context is the difference between effectiveness and ineffectiveness. It is the difference between pleasing the Lord and displeasure. It is the difference between effective and lasting warfare versus limited ineffective warfare. Jesus paid a huge price for us. If our doctrine is confused, we will think salvation depends on us when in fact Jesus already paid that price. If righteousness could be gained through human effort before or after salvation, Christ died in vain. Do not be quick to take sides. This is the tactic of the enemy to divide God's people. There is no law side or grace side. There is only what God is doing today versus what God was doing in the past. God is the designer and this is how we are saved and operate today. There is no hyper grace involved in the true gospel of grace. Talk about these things openly and never fear appearing vulnerable. Your decision to appear vulnerable is strength. In order to be conformed to the image of Christ, we must believe right. It is not by human effort but by the power of the gospel. If you went through any of the things that were described God is trying to get your attention. God wants a purified people. God wants unity amongst the body of Christ. Religion is a waste of time and effort concerning living a life that pleases God. Faith pleases God. Faith in God's word is pleasing. Religion is of the flesh. It does no good to anybody desiring to have an authentic relationship with God. There is only one way to have an authentic relationship with God and that is through humility that comes from knowing you cannot do anything to make God do anything. He decided to love you and lavish grace on you because He is good. He decided to say all the promises are yours if you believe. God is not good to us because we are good. God is good to us because God is good. You can walk in freedom knowing Christ is sufficient and take your relationship with God to a new level. There are many new levels that God can take you. If you were ever to be a leader one day in an important position, you would need God's grace. If you made one mistake, you would be attacked relentlessly by society in an attempt to unstable your mind and get you to quit whatever God has called you to. Your relationship with God is no different. How can a man who listens to the accusations of the devil stand firm in the sufficiency of Christ if he never settled that in his heart? You have to be mentally strong. You get your strength from the Lord. How can we reign and rule in life through Jesus Christ if we do not understand that we are complete in him? Do we reign in life until we mess up? His grace is sufficient. The Holy Spirit will teach you and guide you in the relationship with God. If we want to inherit the earth, we must do it by God's power through the truth of his word.

ABOUT THE AUTHOR

Randy Randles is an author who lives in Central California. He has educational degrees in Bachelor's in Management and Master's in Sport Management. His job includes customer service and basketball coaching. Randy has been a believer of Jesus Christ for years. He has great passion to continue to understand the word of God and help believers in all aspects of the Christian walk. During his free time for hobbies he likes to play basketball and spend time with family.